Contents

Preface

FOR SOME TIME, many teachers have felt the need for a series of handbooks designed for ordinary teachers in ordinary classrooms. So many books seem to be written for privileged teachers in privileged environments–teachers with large classrooms, large budgets for expensive equipment, and small classes.

Most of us are not so lucky: most teachers are short of almost everything except students. They have little time for elaborate theories and time-consuming classroom routines. In particular, they don't have time for long books full of complicated jargon.

Longman Keys to Language Teaching have been written especially for the ordinary teacher. The books offer sound, practical, down-to-earth advice on basic techniques and approaches in the classroom. Most of the suggested activities can be adapted and used for almost any class, by any teacher.

This book, *Effective Class Management*, focuses on the organisational aspects of teaching English successfully. It contains a lot of useful advice to the teacher: it includes good ways of organising work in the classroom, and useful guidelines on making the most of one's time and resources. This book will be particularly useful for teachers who are just starting their careers, or for those who wish to rethink their approaches to teaching.

Author's note

I should like to record my gratitude to everyone who has helped me to produce this book. In particular, I should like to thank John Underwood, who suggested many practical teaching ideas. I am grateful, too, to the many teachers from all around the world who have been willing to discuss their work with me and who have made me think carefully about the practicalities of successful language teaching.

Mary Underwood
London
June 1987

Know yourself

Almost everyone in the world has met at least one teacher and has a view on 'teachers'. But what sort of person is a good teacher?

Teachers, like everyone else, have a variety of abilities and skills and need to make the best possible use of whatever talents they have. This chapter aims to help you identify the things you are good at and to suggest ways of using your particular abilities. It focuses on language ability, personal talents, knowledge and teaching skills.

Language

Obviously, being a fluent, accurate English speaker is a great help, but this alone does not make you into a successful teacher. Indeed, many really good teachers of English are people whose own command of the language is quite limited. This is because they frequently understand their students' difficulties better than native speakers of the language do. If you are not a native speaker, the secret lies in being confident about the English you do use and not being embarrassed about your lack of greater knowledge. Sometimes your students will ask you: 'What's the English for . . . .?' and you may not know the answer. Don't worry! It's far better to say 'I don't know, but I'll find out for you' than to try to avoid answering the question. (Isn't it strange how language teachers feel they should know every word in the language they are teaching even though there are many words in their own native language which they don't know!) Of course, teachers go on learning more through-out their careers, but it's far more important to work on the 'quality' of the language you use and want to teach your students first of all. There are lots of ways non-native teachers can develop their own language skills:

1 *In private*

Think about the language you might need and check through the part of the book you are going to use for a particular lesson. Make sure you are familiar with the language in the book, then speak the words/phrases/sentences aloud (in private!) so that you can hear how you sound. It's important to speak out clearly, not just whisper. You will then find that your speech in class will be more confident and more easily understood. You will also discover if there are words which you have difficulty in pronouncing. Then you can try to get them right yourself before going to your class. If there is a cassette to be used with your book, listen to the recording too, as this can often be a help with pronunciation. It's particularly worthwhile doing this kind of 'rehearsal' for things that you are likely to say regularly–'Listen carefully,' 'Turn to page X,' 'Write this down,' 'Look at the picture,' 'Be quiet please,' 'Very good,' 'Well done.' If you possibly can, get someone to check that you are saying these things accurately and clearly.

2 *In groups*

If you are working with other teachers of English, it's a good idea to have regular meetings to help each other with this kind of preparation. Just look ahead two or three days and check that you can handle the language you need for your next few lessons. A Head of Department might call the meetings (which can be as short as fifteen minutes). If not, any group of teachers can get together on a 'self-help' basis. They will soon discover that each can gain something from the experience.

3 *With help*

Clearly groups of teachers which include native speakers of English have an advantage when practising spoken language. Other groups may have collections of recordings by native speakers which may prove useful. It may be possible in an area with lots of teachers of English to form groups 'across schools'. In this way those teaching, say, Form 2 will be able to 'rehearse' with others working at the same level.

There may well already be a teachers' club or teachers' centre in your area. If so, why not suggest that each meeting includes a fifteen-minute language 'clinic' when teachers can check up on anything they are unsure of by asking colleagues/experts (in private, or in small groups, to avoid embarrassment)?

Talents

It's sometimes said that teachers are really people who wanted to be actors or other performers but failed! Whilst this is probably rarely the case, there are clearly advantages in having some of the qualities of a good performer–a clear voice, good presentation, self-confidence. And even if your acting skills are limited, there may be other things that you are good at which you have never thought of applying to your teaching. Why not check and see what talents you have which you could make better use of?

Can you sing or play a musical instrument?

It's useful to be able to sing or play music, as people the world over enjoy music and song. Playing a small, portable instrument is ideal because you can bring it to the class or the language club whenever you like. Getting your students to predict the end of some of the lines of a song is good practice as well as being fun. Asking more advanced students to help you write a song which you will then put to music (if you can!) is enjoyable. If that's too difficult, your students will enjoy just singing along with you and learning some of the words of the English songs you know.

If you are not a musician and you can't sing very well, you can still have an occasional song in your class by playing a tape or a record and singing along with the recording. Many people would find it difficult to lead the singing themselves, but very few would be incapable of joining in and encouraging others to sing. Why not give it a try?

Can you draw?

Most teachers would not claim to be artists, but sooner or later every teacher has to draw something on the board. Drawings can be used as a way of presenting new language and explaining new vocabulary, and you don't need to be an expert to do this. Probably the three most important 'rules' are:

1 Keep it simple.
2 Try it out in advance.
3 Draw it big enough to be seen.

If you have an overhead projector or a large flip chart available, things are made easier for you as you can prepare your drawings in advance (even copying them or tracing them–if they are big enough–from books). With a bit of practice even the least artistic

Simple drawings on a flip chart

teacher can produce drawings which are perfectly adequate for learning purposes.

Can you act?

Maybe the question should really be 'Are you willing to try to act?' It's not necessary to be able to portray the major characters from classical plays (although you may wish to do that kind of thing). But it is helpful if you can occasionally pretend to be someone else without feeling (and therefore looking) foolish. You may wish to read a dialogue, for example. It is much more convincing if you can use different voices to indicate changes of speaker. Even if you only change the loudness or speed or pitch of your voice a little, you can make the contrast between speakers clear.

If you decide that the class will do a role play activity as part of a lesson, it is much more encouraging for your students if you are willing to take part or to show them the kind of thing you expect. You might for example want your class to do role play in pairs. Person A is to be the shop assistant. Person B is the angry customer who has come to return, say, a pair of faulty shoes. You could begin by taking the part of the angry customer yourself and showing how anger can be expressed. (If you do this, choose the student to play Person A carefully. Some students might feel threatened in this situation.) It may be worth pointing out that anger can be expressed without shouting, so that your classroom won't become too noisy when all the students try the role play at the same time! You could then do the role play again with another member of the class, this time taking the part of the shop assistant and demonstrating how someone in this position can show calmness, consideration, politeness, firmness, etc. This kind of thing does not demand great acting skills, but it does need you to be willing to take part. It is unreasonable to expect your students to do things that you are not willing to do yourself, but it is perfectly acceptable to say 'I'm not very good at this, but I'll try.'

Specialist knowledge

Many people who teach English also teach another subject. Indeed lots of teachers spend much more of their time teaching their 'first' subject than teaching English. This means that these teachers, who often do their English teaching to the lower forms of a school, have specialist knowledge in some other field. And those teachers whose major expertise is in English often have a particular knowledge of an aspect of English: for example literature, history, or geography.

There is no doubt that students like to have interesting content in their language lessons, so it is important to maximise the use you make of your knowledge by introducing facts and ideas as they seem appropriate. In this way you will ensure that your students experience language being used for a real, communicative purpose, i.e. the transmission of knowledge. They will not be limited to the somewhat artificial world created by language coursebook writers. If the coursebook lacks interesting content, you can supplement it by adding some more stimulating material from other sources. There are possibilities in practically all subjects normally included in the curriculum, though the easiest source to handle is probably your own specialist subject area. Consider, for example:

Geography

Maps are a really good resource for language work. For lower level learners you may want to draw your own simplified maps. With advanced classes you will be able to use the atlases provided for geography classes.

Weather charts, population charts, charts showing levels of industry, income, vegetation, etc. can all be used effectively. For example, they can be used for the practice of colours, numbers, comparatives, tenses, or for learning sets of new words. Classes can produce wall-charts, individuals can draw their own charts, teachers can provide charts from which other work is derived.

Projects can focus on the geography of a particular country or region, or on the local area around the school.

History

Family trees can be produced and discussed. And they can form the basis of a range of learning activities: for example, the vocabulary of family relationships, 'who' questions, comparatives and superlatives can all be practised using the data from a family tree. Family names can be traced back. Stories can be read and told about historical characters and events.

A project can be based on the historical development of the local town or a company which operates in the town. Finding out about famous people who lived in the region and writing the stories of their lives can be undertaken by groups of students.

Producing a history of the school provides opportunities for students to conduct interviews, make notes, write paragraphs, collect pictures, etc., and leads to a collaborative exercise in producing the final document.

Mathematics

Some of the problems of calculation can be used in English lessons: adding up bills, working out income, writing out number sequences, etc. Puzzles are always fun, so you might introduce some number puzzles into your lessons.

It's probably easiest to involve your students in number work in the English lesson by using activities which are personally relevant to them, for example: 'If you had (£1000) given to you today, what would you do with it?' You could suggest what you would do yourself – 'I'd give half to charity, I'd spend (£100) on buying...'. (Use the local currency.) There are sometimes units or exercises in coursebooks which are about money or distance or time, and when these occur the 'mathematics and English' teacher can take the opportunity to introduce more examples.

Science

There are few scientific topics in English coursebooks, perhaps because most English coursebook writers are from non-scientific backgrounds. Nevertheless you can search out the opportunities that do exist and use your own knowledge to supplement your coursebook. You might tell the story of a scientific discovery, or get your students to read a recent report on space travel. You could demonstrate a well-known (simple) scientific phenomenon.

Whatever part of the curriculum you select topics from, it is important to get the agreement and support of your colleagues, especially if you think you might be duplicating work they might do with the class. And you should take every opportunity to make your students aware of the interrelationships between their English studies and the various other subjects in the curriculum.

General knowledge of an English-speaking country

The specialist English teacher probably knows more about one of the English-speaking countries than teachers with other specialisms, and this too can be exploited.

You can 'bring to life' one of the environments in which English is spoken by talking (often from first-hand experience) about the place, the people and the customs. If you have been to an English-speaking country, you may have brought things home which will be of interest to your students – photos, posters, books, souvenirs, programmes, newspapers, postcards. Even if your students are unlikely ever to go abroad themselves, their enjoyment of the language can be increased by using the 'realia' which you can bring to the lessons, and making comparisons with similar things in the students' own environment. You might consider the differences between advertisements in the English-speaking country and locally; look at photos and other pictures and compare the clothes, the scenery, the houses, the public buildings; examine the differences in transport – trains, buses, cars, road-signs, etc.

'Realia' from a visit to England

All of these 'inputs' must, of course, be presented in a form and at a level appropriate to the learners. Teachers sometimes treat students who are unsophisticated in their use of the foreign language as lacking in sophistication in all other spheres. This is clearly not the case and many language learners can consider and discuss complex matters provided that they are expressed in simple language.

Teaching skills

Before you can begin to use your talents and your knowledge effectively in class, you may need to spend a little time considering your basic teaching skills and improving your performance in any area where you feel you are weak. In fact, you are probably more skilled than you think, but there may be certain areas where you can do even better. Really good classroom performance on your part will have a significant effect on the way in which your students see you. This, in turn, will have an effect on their behaviour. Consider, for example:

Reading aloud

- Do you read clearly and loudly enough?
- Do you stumble over difficult words?
- Is your intonation good?
- Do you sound as if you care about what you're reading?

You can certainly improve your reading by practising in the manner already suggested on page 8, and by listening to other people who are good readers (perhaps on the radio). It is often a good idea to practise any piece you're going to use in your next lesson by reading it (aloud) the evening before.

Writing on the board

- Is your board work well organised (or is the board a mess by the end of your lesson)?
- Is your writing legible?
- Can you write reasonably quickly on the board?

Again, practice is the answer. After just two or three twenty-minute sessions you will see a significant improvement in your board work if you are self-critical about your efforts.

A good practice session might follow this pattern:

1 Be sure the board is as clean as you can make it.

2 Write out the beginning of a letter on the board (your address top right, the date beneath it, 'Dear . . .' to the left, the beginning of the first paragraph).

3 Look critically at your effort (or, better still, get someone else to comment on it).
   - Are the lines of writing reasonably straight?
   - Are there any letters which you form badly?
   - Does your writing get smaller/bigger as you go on?
   - Are your capital letters clear?
   - Have you written over any letters without wiping the incorrect letters off the board first?
   - Does the whole thing look like a letter?
   - Can it all be read easily from the sides and back of the class?

4 If you think you could improve on your first attempt, try again and take another critical look.

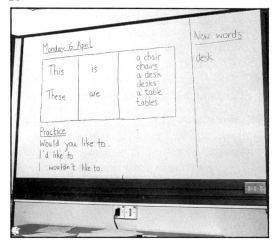
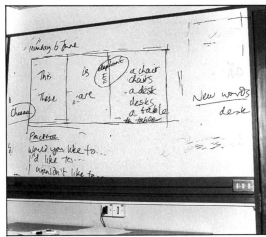

Board work – good and bad

5 Clean the board well again and then write out a table:

I We You	like	eating singing working	at the office at school at home

6 Criticise your effort using the questions in (3) above, and asking yourself also:

- Are the lines reasonably straight?
- Are the choices clear?

7 Try again if necessary.

8 Clean the board thoroughly again, and write six lines of continuous prose (copy something from this book if you wish), working quite quickly.

9 Carry out the same critical appraisal and see whether writing more quickly has caused you to write less well.

10 Write a few more lines and try to decide what is a reasonably 'safe' speed for you.

Obviously you'll want to do this kind of practice in private or with a sympathetic friend or colleague. It really is worth doing it, as good board work is not only helpful to your learners but also contributes to a happy class environment. (Have you ever been irritated by something written so badly that people need to keep asking what it's meant to be?) In Chapter 8, page 81, you will find a few 'rules' which will help you to make your use of the board as a teaching aid more effective.

Using equipment

- Are you happy using machines (cassette recorders, overhead projectors, etc.)?
- Can you 'load' the machines quickly and correctly?
- Do you know what to do if they don't work?

Teachers who go on training courses are often shown how to use equipment, but by the time they come to use it for themselves they find they are not sure what to do. The best time to get to know a particular piece of equipment really well is in the week or two before you are going to use it. The best way to learn is by 'hands on' experience. The quickest way is by having someone explain it and demonstrate it to you, and then by going through the various steps yourself a number of times. If the instruction manual is available, you should read this carefully too. If there's nobody available to show you how a machine works, you will have to depend on the instruction manual alone and go through it all step by step. If you are unlucky enough to have nobody to help you and no instruction book available, you may be able to work it out for yourself but, in the last resort, you can always write to the manufacturer and ask for a copy of the instruction manual.

One practice session is not enough. It is important to follow up the first attempt by two or three further sessions to check that you have mastered the method and to develop 'fluency' in using the equipment. Again, some quiet private practice is called for. Have you ever seen a teacher trying to position an overhead projector in a class when he or she hasn't mastered it? Have you seen a teacher trying to thread a film or load slides when he or she is unsure of how to do it? Not only does the teacher get hot and flustered, but he or she often loses the respect of the students, who believe that teachers ought to be able to do these things.

Attitude to discipline

Discipline is, of course, an important matter for teachers in schools and one which is worth giving some thought to. A number of questions come to mind:

- How do you maintain order in your class?
- How much noise do you consider 'tolerable'?
- What do you believe is unacceptable behaviour?
- Do you punish students who misbehave?

If you work in a school, there are almost certainly some agreed policies on discipline. You will be expected to follow these, but when you are actually with a group in a classroom you have considerable freedom as far as discipline is concerned. Nobody can tell you exactly what to do on every kind of occasion. You need to have considered your own attitudes and decided roughly what is and is not acceptable, and you need to have an idea of how you will react to various kinds of misbehaviour. It is important to try to be fair, and not to punish a misdeed severely on one occasion while ignoring it on another. It is far better, of course, to avoid situations which may lead to misbehaviour. Students who are busy and believe that what they are doing is worthwhile are less likely to be disruptive. And a well-organised teacher is less likely to have problems with discipline.

Opportunities for self development

By thinking critically about yourself – your language level, your talents, your knowledge, your teaching skills – you may have identified aspects of your performance as a teacher which you want to improve, and you may now wish to look for opportunities for self development. Have you thought of:

joining a language club (or even starting one)? ☐

attending language improvement classes? ☐

attending classes in art/music/drama? ☐

joining a local library? ☐

arranging to work with one or two English teacher colleagues
to improve your performance? ☐

finding out what local organisations exist and asking what they
can do to help you? ☐

reading other books about teaching? ☐

Tick any two which you think are worth doing and which you feel you *can* do. Why not do something about it right now?

Know your school

This chapter focuses on things you should know about, not just to avoid problems, but also because they might contribute quite significantly to your success and happiness as a teacher. It deals with the 'philosophy' of the school; the attitudes and interests of the other teachers; who is responsible for what; your own responsibilities and rights; and the normal pattern of behaviour of staff.

Note that 'school' is used in this chapter, and elsewhere, to mean school/college/institute or whatever.

The 'philosophy' of the school

Schools range from very formal organisations with strict discipline to very casual organisations where discipline is not considered important. Heads and Principals range from authoritarian to permissive. And of course you may have a Head of Department or colleagues who do not always comply with the overall philosophy of the school.

What about where *you* work? It's important to think about the type of school you are in and to adjust your own behaviour accordingly. You might, for example, have the idea one day of getting one of your English classes to carry out a survey of the interests of teachers in the school. But you should not ask them to do this if your colleagues believe that students should not bother them during their free time or that this kind of activity encourages students to be over-familiar with their teachers. If your fellow teachers hold these views you should not risk putting your students and yourself in such a difficult position.

If the general philosophy of the school means that students are expected to remain silent in class unless spoken to by the teacher, you will have to be careful about how much noise your classes make. On the other hand, you cannot do your job properly if you require your students to be silent. It is important, therefore, to try to convey tactfully to your colleagues (and, most of all, to the Principal) that in order to learn to speak English and understand the spoken language, your students will need to make some noise. (Nobody expects the singing class to be conducted in silence, do they?) Clearly you must be in control of the class, but group and pair work will cause some noise. You might consider inviting the Principal and other colleagues to attend one or two of your lessons. If they came, they might be persuaded that the activity is so obviously useful that the level of noise is acceptable.

If you are unsure about what the philosophy of your school is, you may find it safer to keep your teaching style rather formal until you learn more about how other teachers work. It is easier to relax your approach as time goes on rather than to become more formal with your students. Of course, this doesn't mean that you should adopt an unfriendly manner. It is a question of the degree of informality you permit and the extent to which you let things pass rather than take action to control them.

Attitudes to discipline are greatly influenced by the culture of the country in which you are working and the culture of the students you are teaching. It is important to respect the 'norms' of the environment in which you are working and not to try to impose your own system. Once you have become accepted as a colleague by other members of staff, you may then perhaps suggest ideas which they can consider and possibly adopt.

Other teachers' attitudes

Whilst *you* may feel that English is a particularly important part of the curriculum, you should not be surprised to discover that most teachers of other subjects do not share your view. On the other hand, you may find a small number who, whilst giving priority to their own subjects, are quite interested in what the students are doing in their English lessons. If so, you might be able to foster this interest and use it to the advantage of your students. You could:

- offer to teach your class a song in English (perhaps in collaboration with the music teacher);
- agree with the geography teacher that, in an English lesson, you will go through part of a geography lesson which has already been done in the students' own language–using a map, for example, and talking about the regions of a country (see page 12);

ENGLISH CLUB

LUNCHTIME FUN

Pop music quiz. Bring your favourite record / cassette and three questions to ask about it.

Main Hall, 13.00 hours

☆ SURPRISE PRIZES ♩♩♩ ☆

An invitation to an 'English' event

- ask the art teacher if your class can work on an art project related to an English-speaking country and offer to supply the necessary background information and language;
- offer to organise pen-friends–not only for those students who are studying English;
- prepare an occasional 'English' event to which you invite some or all of the rest of the school. Just a half-hour event with, for example, such things as recitations, songs, dances, a slide-show, or games;
- plan combined outings/trips with teachers of other subjects when relevant opportunities occur (e.g. to see an exhibition of paintings by an English artist).

All of these activities increase the awareness of English in the school. More importantly, they help your students to appreciate that understanding and speaking a foreign language is not something 'separate' and 'irrelevant', but rather a useful skill with close links with many other activities which they enjoy.

The extent of your responsibilities

If you have been teaching in one school for some time, you will have gradually found out who is responsible for various things. New teachers will have to get to know the extent of their responsibilities and a senior English teacher must be sure that responsibilities are shared among the teaching team.

A list of some areas of responsibility is given below. The column on the right of the list is for you to put in the name of the person responsible for each thing in your school.

Area of responsibility	Name of person
The selection and acquisition of books and other materials	_____
The organisation/distribution of materials	_____
The preparation of the syllabus	_____
The preparation of schemes of work (i.e. the division of the syllabus into sections to be covered in various years, terms or months)	_____
The organisation of students into classes	_____
The management of audio-visual equipment	_____
The management of audio-visual materials	_____
The co-ordination of reports	_____
The writing of test and examination questions	_____
The conduct of tests and examinations	_____
The selection of students for external examinations	_____
The promotion of teachers	_____
The in-service training of new teachers	_____

The general pattern of staff behaviour

There are lots of small things that teachers who have been in a particular school for years take for granted, but which relative newcomers need to notice and remember. Can you answer these questions about your school?

- What is the usual form of address for students–first names/family names/both?
- Are there any 'rules' about suitable dress for teachers in your school?
- Is it normal practice for each teacher to clean the board at the end of each lesson?
- What schemes of work are you required to prepare? Who are you required to give them to/where are you required to keep them?
- Are you expected to write out your lesson plans in a particular form?
- Are you required to keep your lesson plans for others to look at?
- How often is homework normally given?
- How much homework should be given?
- How is the collecting and returning of homework arranged?
- What system is used for recording marks? Are weekly/monthly/termly records needed?
- What must you do if you are unable to go to school one day?
- What is *your* responsibility if another teacher is absent?
- What must you do if you feel ill and need to leave your class?
- What must you do if a student becomes ill or has an accident during your lesson?
- What punishments are you allowed to give?
- Are you allowed to write letters directly to parents, or must they go through the Principal?
- Where must you put notes you wish to leave for other teachers or for students?
- How are school reports organised? Are they required monthly/termly/yearly?
- What information, in what detail, is expected on school reports?

If you are not sure about the answers to any of the questions, you could probably find out more by talking to a colleague who has been at the school longer than you have. Once you have established the facts, you may find that one or two of the answers could be exploited as part of your English-teaching work. The collecting and returning of homework, for example, might be organised by students, thus giving extra opportunities for real language use. Even the punishments you give to students who misbehave can be designed to produce more English practice! Opportunities to generate the real use of English shouldn't be missed. This is particularly important in schools in non-English-speaking countries where the use of English outside the classroom is likely to be very limited.

Parts of this chapter are relevant for teachers of all subjects, not just for teachers of English, but they are important aspects of a teacher's life and greatly affect the status of your subject in the school. This in turn affects what you can achieve. In addition, understanding the system can save you a lot of time and trouble and leave you free to devote more energy to the actual teaching/learning process.

Look again at the three lists in this chapter (pages 20–21, 22, and 23).

1 **From the first list (pages 20–21), select something you can do to increase awareness of English in your school.**

2 **From the second list (page 22), identify the area of responsibility which you think you should know more about and arrange to discuss it with the appropriate colleague.**

3 **Find out any answers you don't already know to questions on the third list (page 23).**

If there are other questions about the general pattern of staff behaviour which you can't answer, ask colleagues about those matters too.

Know your students

It is often said that adults feel nervous and ill at ease when they join a language class and are even quite frightened when asked to speak. Attention is drawn less frequently to the fact that many children may experience the same kind of reticence and fear. Whether you teach adults or children, your approach, especially in the early stages of a course, will be a major factor in overcoming any lack of confidence on the students' part. Learners of all ages should be treated with care and respect. Knowing your students by name, knowing their backgrounds and interests, knowing about their previous language-learning experiences and their attitudes to English will enable you to help them to learn more happily and effectively.

Names

Being able to address students by name has considerable advantages both for the teacher and the students. From the teacher's point of view, it avoids all kinds of confusion which might arise in identifying who should be responding; it generates a friendly relationship with the students; it is the natural way to attract somebody's attention; it speeds up the organising of pair and group work. From the students' point of view, it produces a more secure atmosphere.

Even if you believe that you are not very good at remembering, it *is* possible to get to know your students by name. Having established what the normal form of address is for students in your school, try one of these methods:

1 Ask the students to write their names on pieces of folded paper/ card which they can stand up on the front of their desks at every English lesson until you know everyone's name. (If the students don't already know each other, this method helps them too, but it obviously works best for them when all the students are seated in such a way that they face each other.)

Using name cards

2 Buy cheap labels and ask the students to print their names on the labels in large letters and wear them. (Sticky envelope labels are adequate, but only last for one lesson.)

3 Draw a plan of the classroom and write in the names of the students. Ask the students to sit in the same seats at each lesson, at least for the first few weeks. Keep the plan on your desk during lessons until you know all the names.

4 If your school asks students to provide photographs of themselves and you can make copies of them, label the photos and learn the names at home.

In some schools, students are given an English name just for use in their English classes. They either use the English equivalent of their own names or, if there is no equivalent, any English name they like. Many young people don't know any English names, so you need to have a list and help them to choose one, if your English department uses this system. Some people think there is no point in giving students English names. Others believe that there may even be serious disadvantages: for example, students may not respond to their newly-acquired name at first, whereas they will respond automatically when they hear their own, familiar name.

Using an invented name may give students a feeling that there is something artificial about the English class and that they are not 'being themselves' when speaking English.

You may not be able to choose whether to introduce English names or not. If there is a policy about this in your school, you will need to comply, although you might consider raising the matter for discussion with your colleagues. If you are free to choose, you should make up your mind before starting to teach a particular class, as it would cause considerable confusion to change everyone's name in the middle of the course!

Backgrounds

It is helpful to know something about your students' backgrounds. Language classes give teachers many more opportunities to discover details about their students' lives than most other classes. It is, however, very important that class activities don't lead you (or the students) to pry into anyone's background and don't force students to reveal things about themselves which they do not wish to reveal. With some classes it may be worth explaining (in the students' first language if necessary) that you do not wish to pry. You should also tell the students that avoiding giving information which one does not want to give is a useful communicative skill!

A good basic principle is never to ask your students in class anything that you would not wish to be asked yourself. Even then, you might still cause embarrassment quite by accident. It is sometimes helpful, particularly with school students, to know of any special circumstances (e.g. a family tragedy or a financial problem) so that you can try to protect individuals from hurt or embarrassment. It's possible that a school would keep such information on confidential student records. If you are allowed to, you should check these records so that you can avoid upsetting anyone in your lessons.

Interests

Your students will find their English lessons more stimulating if some of their English work is concerned with things that interest them, so you will want to find out what these things are.

Almost any hobby which a student has can be incorporated into an English lesson. It's hard to imagine a student's passionate interest in collecting butterflies being of any use in a history lesson, but in the English class it can become, if only briefly, the focal point of an activity. A student could bring his or her collection to class and tell the rest of the class about all the different species. A question and answer session could centre around the collection. Students could discuss whether it is ethical to collect butterflies. They could also write about making collections of other things. The collection could form the basis of practice for adjectives, comparatives, superlatives, question forms, past tenses and so on.

Whilst collecting butterflies may be a rare hobby, some interests are more commonly shared. Do you know what most of your students are interested in? Is it football, clothes, pop music, sport, films, television?

One way of getting the information you want is to organise a pair work activity. For this you would need to produce a large chart, like the one started below, which the students would fill in. The chart should be large enough and clear enough to be stuck on the wall or board, either before it is filled in or when everyone has finished writing information on it.

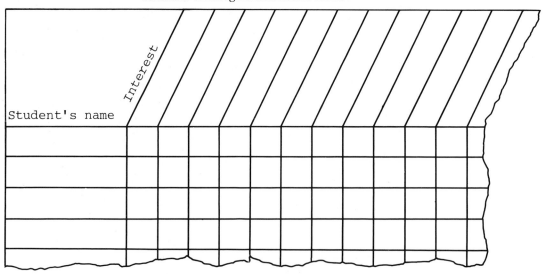

PROCEDURE:

1 Show the class the chart and ask for suggestions to put in the 'Interest' boxes, e.g. football, dancing, playing the guitar. Do not

attempt to fill in all the 'Interest' boxes at this stage. You may
need to write the list on the board as well as on the chart, as the
class may not be able to read it from the chart.

2 Explain that students must work in pairs as nobody is allowed to
complete the chart for him/herself.

3 Each person must discover the *three* things which his/her partner
is most interested in and make a note of them.

4 When they have finished, each person records his/her partner's
interests on the chart by entering the name and ticking the
appropriate boxes.

Previous experience of learning English

If you are going to teach a class which has been learning English
in a lower form in your school, you will want to find out what they
have already learned. There may be an official written record of
what has been taught at each level which you can consult. You
will be able to look through the book(s) they used and talk to their
previous teacher(s). Discussion with the class's previous teachers
is most important as they will be able to tell you the strengths
and weaknesses of the particular group. They will also be able to
describe the kinds of learning experience which the group has had.
All this will help you to build up a picture of your new class.

Sometimes, however, you will find that the class is different from
what your colleagues have told you. It is important then to stick
to your own judgement. Students do change. It may be that, for a
variety of reasons, the students are more lively (or less so), more
articulate (or less so), more disciplined (or less so) than you have
been led to believe. This doesn't mean that those who taught the
class before were mistaken in their views. It simply means that the
class, or individuals within it, have changed–hopefully for the
better!

You may, however, be in a position where you are the first person
in your school to teach a particular group. Again, you may well
have a clear syllabus which you must follow. The emphasis you
give to this or that part will depend on whether your students are
all complete beginners or whether some of them have had previous
experience of learning English (or perhaps another language).

There is little point in asking a class of young students questions like 'Have you studied the Past Perfect?' or 'Can you express regret?' The only way to establish what is already known may be to start with a diagnostic test to discover what your new students can and cannot do. Unfortunately, doing this can sometimes simply add to the pressure already felt by those who have not enjoyed or not done well in English. It may be worth managing with less knowledge of your students' previous learning of English in the interests of creating a good relationship with them. You will want to make them feel that they are going to do something really interesting and to enjoy their lessons with you. A test may not give this impression! You can, however, talk to the class (in their own language if necessary) about their previous experience – 'When did you start learning English?' 'Did you use a book?' 'What was it called?' You can then do a quick revision of the things they have already learned by giving them some short check tests. Be sure the students understand that these tests are only to help you decide what gaps they have in their knowledge, so that you can help them to fill the gaps (and, of course, you must not forget to do just that).

It is not easy to know how much time should be devoted to this kind of revision/diagnosis. Too much leads to boredom both for those who can and those who cannot do the tests. Too little may give you an erroneous picture of the students' capabilities. In general, it's probably best to do too little rather than too much, and, as most learners want to 'get on with the book', it's best to inter-sperse this revision with the first few units of the coursebook you are using.

Attitudes to English

'It's too difficult.'
'I'll never need English anyway.'
'It's stupid. I feel silly trying to speak.'
'It's boring.'

'It'll be useful for a job.'
'I like English pop music.'
'I want to go to America, so I must speak English.'
'Everyone has to speak English.'

How did *you* feel when you started to learn another language? Do you remember? Your attitude was probably more influenced by the teacher you had than by whether you actually wanted or did not want to learn English.

There is absolutely no doubt that the enthusiasm and skill of the teacher has an enormous effect on the attitudes of learners. You will want to share your own fascination with the language with your students. You may have a story to tell about how you got so involved in English. You may want to tell your class what your knowledge of English has meant to you. There may be English-speaking people in the country in which you are teaching, and talking about their achievements may arouse the interest of your class. There may be natives of the country who, through their knowledge of English, have been able to influence events in the world. There could be very practical reasons for your particular students to learn English – perhaps because they live in a tourist area, perhaps because English is an important language used in secondary or tertiary education, perhaps because they are in an international school overseas.

English on signs around the world

You may have things to show your students which might spark off their interest – photos, books, magazines, music, letters and so on. Posters and wall-charts add to the atmosphere and remind students that the subject has a great deal to do with life outside the classroom. You could invite your students to bring anything with English words on it into class one day and use the realia as a motivating force. Or your students could produce a list of all the

English words they see in the street or in shops, noting where each one is:

Word	Where seen
stop	on a road sign

If the list would not be ridiculously long, you could put it up on the wall in the class and help the students to add to it.

It is not only at the beginning (although first impressions *are* very important) that positive attitudes to learning English need to be fostered. After what is, we hope, the initial excitement of beginning to learn a language, there is almost always a stage when students reach a 'plateau', when they begin to feel that they are not making any progress. At this point you need to find new ways of motivating your classes and making it all seem worthwhile. For example, you could use an English programme from the radio, or a map of the world on which to identify all the countries where English is spoken, or a recording of an English song, or, if your school is lucky enough to have the facilities, a video or a film. Pen-friends and trips abroad also play a significant part in maintaining motivation. Where such steps are impracticable, it is even more important for the teacher to seize every opportunity to make the learning of English 'meaningful' for the students.

Whatever facilities are available, and in some situations they may be very few indeed, it is the lively, purposeful class atmosphere with plenty to do which will do most to maintain positive attitudes. It is the skill and enthusiasm of the teacher which will be the most important factor in keeping the students motivated. If you ever doubt this, think back to your own favourite teacher when you were a student and consider what it was that made his or her classes so special.

Keeping records

In addition to being a help when you are teaching, knowing about your students is also helpful when you have to write reports or references for them. If you have a lot of students, it is worthwhile keeping a notebook in which you can build up 'profiles' by jotting down bits of information which you think useful. Some teachers allocate a page per student, and so provide themselves with a handy record to refer back to. Or you may have space to do this in the book in which you record marks, examination results, etc.

Look back at the headings in this chapter and think for a few minutes about each one in relation to *your* students. You may like to write a short 'Programme for Action' for yourself using the chart below.

Class	What I need to know more about	How I'm going to find out	When

Finally, if you feel that you can't do all the things suggested in this chapter because you have so much to do already, then give priority to learning your students' names. It is so much easier to control and organise the class if you know everyone's name. Do go back to the four suggestions on pages 25–26, and if you have not been in the habit of learning your students' names in the past, decide which method suits you best (or think of another one) and resolve to address every student by name from now on.

An encouraging class atmosphere

Some practical ways of maintaining motivation were described in Chapter 3. Here, we consider ways in which the general atmosphere in the class can assist learning and how the behaviour and language of both teacher and students can contribute to this atmosphere. (Chapter 5 deals with the physical environment of the classroom and the effect this can have on your students.)

In this chapter you are invited to consider:

- how a happy, purposeful, supportive atmosphere can be achieved;
- how to ensure that English is spoken whenever possible;
- how to balance fluency and accuracy;
- how to make your own language appropriate to the level of the class;
- how to give encouragement to your students;
- how to involve all your students, in, for example, question and answer sessions;
- the place of examinations and tests;
- the contribution 'out-of-class' activities might make to your students' learning – libraries, clubs, etc.

Giving a sense of purpose

What makes everyone in the class feel that what they are doing is worthwhile and that they have a part to play in class activities? How can you create this kind of atmosphere?

Here are ten suggestions:

1 Address every student by name and encourage the rest of the class to do so too (see page 25).

2 Always be polite to your students and expect them to be polite to each other as well as to you. (This includes arriving on time and apologising for lateness.)

3 Make sure that you do not show favouritism towards particular students.

4 Plan clearly what you are going to do in each lesson, but do not stick so rigidly to it that you disallow even valid interruptions.

5 Tell the students what you want to achieve in the lesson and then, at the end, say how successful you think you have been.

6 Include every student in some way during each lesson if possible and do not let one or two students monopolise the class.

7 Provide opportunities for the students to talk and listen to each other rather than all communication being between you and them.

8 Say what you mean and mean what you say. If, for example, you have told the class to look at the next unit before the next lesson *if they have time*, do not complain if some students have not done so. But if you say 'This homework must be done by Monday,' and some students do not do it, then you must be firm and express your displeasure. As far as a purposeful class is concerned, the firmness of your disapproval is an important part of your relationship with the group.

9 Do the things which you have told the students you will do. (e.g. 'I'll bring it and show it to you at our next lesson.') If you are bad at remembering, keep a notebook in which to write reminders to yourself.

10 Be consistent in how you deal with your students. If you have said that certain behaviour is not acceptable (e.g. eating in class), then you must enforce the 'rules'. Simple but firm insistence is best–'Carlos, please don't eat in class; it's unpleasant for the rest of the class.' Sometimes you will have to be sterner with misbehavers, but if you treat all students alike, your firm stand will not spoil your relationship with the group.

Ensuring that English is spoken

How can you ensure that English is the language of communication in the classroom?

First and foremost, it is important to use English yourself as the normal language of communication and to do this from the very first meeting with a new class, making it plain to your students that you want to conduct the whole lesson in English. It is also a good idea to get into the habit of addressing your students in English whenever possible when you meet them outside the class.

From the beginning, you can use the classroom environment as a topic which your students can comment on (see Chapter 5, pages 55–57). You may start with simple questions – 'Are you cold?', 'Can you see the board?' – and gradually encourage your students to comment freely without waiting for a question from you. At first, students may have difficulty in conveying their messages, but you should make it clear that you have understood without correcting their mistakes, otherwise nobody will dare to comment in the future. For example, when a student says 'Cold'/'Me cold', you should respond, showing that you have understood, with, perhaps, 'Yes. I'm cold too, Michel. Close the window please, Maria.' You should not immediately correct the speaker with 'Not "Me cold", Michel, "I'm cold." Say "I'm cold."' If your students get their messages over successfully – even if in incorrect English at first – you should make it clear that you have understood so that they will feel inclined to try to communicate again and so, with practice, they will become better and better.

It is kinder not to draw attention to a student who has failed to understand by saying such things as 'Can anyone help Ada?', 'What do I want Ada to do?' as Ada will be made to feel very inadequate and discouraged. It is better to try to move a little closer to the individual and to repeat the request or instruction gently. You might also add more gestures to make your meaning clearer. You should, of course, endeavour only to say things which your students are likely to understand. And be careful to reserve the simpler requests and instructions for those who seem to have most difficulty.

Having told the students that their English lessons are to be conducted in English, you will need to use some techniques for ensuring that this is what actually happens. In general, students will co-operate if they feel that you will help them when they need help and that they will not be made to look foolish in front of their fellow students. Sometimes, however, you will need to persuade individual students to refrain from using their native language. In beginners' classes, when students say something in their native language, you can simply say the same thing in English and ask them to repeat it. Indeed, this is sometimes the way in which students seek help with speaking in English. Alternatively, you can respond in English. 'Oh, you haven't got a book, Luisa. Where's your book?', taking care not to sound unfriendly. If you believe that Luisa can say what she wants to say in English, you might just say 'Pardon, Luisa?' to make it clear that you expect her to speak to you in English. Occasionally, you might say, in a jokey way, 'Sorry. I only understand *English* when I'm in an English class.' If you want to be more formal and firm, you can say simply 'Please speak English, Luisa.'

In adult classes, some teachers introduce the idea of students paying a fine if they speak another language. If you choose to do this, it is probably best to give the fines box to a different student each day, so that you are not the one to enforce the fine and there is a sense of fun about it. With school students a similar effect can be gained by having a 'points' system, but it tends to work less well with younger students as it can lead to arguments.

It's worth bearing in mind that the use of audio-visual aids (including posters, etc. on the walls) can increase the amount and range of English used in the class. Words and expressions which are already known are 'triggered' by images and sounds. This sometimes means that students find it easier than they expect to say what they want to say. They are not hampered by having to search in their overall language store, as it were, for their words. They are prompted, though not necessarily consciously, by what they see or hear around them.

Finally, there is no doubt that the teacher's own confident use of the language has a very great influence on the students' willingness to speak in English and so teachers will want to give the best example they can and provide a good model for their classes.

Balancing fluency and accuracy

As well as ensuring that your students can use their newly learned English correctly, you will want to provide opportunities for them to use the language freely to express their own ideas. In other words, you will wish to provide opportunities for your students to develop both accuracy and fluency.

You will have to balance your encouragement of fluency with the need for accuracy. This will become more important as your students progress through their English course, particularly for those students who have to pass English examinations. It is, however, advisable first of all to establish that contributions from all students are welcome and expected without worrying too much about accuracy. It becomes increasingly difficult to get weaker or reticent students to speak at all if you are too strict about accuracy when they first try to say something. This means that they get even less practice and the gap between them and their fellow students grows even wider.

Many teachers find it useful to identify at the planning stage the parts of the lesson when they will focus on fluency and the parts when they will insist on accuracy. You may, for example, decide that you will have an informal chat stage at the beginning or end of each lesson and that this will be a time when you focus on fluency. You may decide that when using drills you will always insist on accuracy. You should avoid springing a surprise on the class by suddenly beginning to correct everything students say, particularly just after a relaxed period of the lesson when fluency has been the focus. It's a good idea to announce your intention – 'In this lesson, I want to concentrate on the "s" on verbs like "he lives", "she goes", "he sings", "she tries". I want you to be extra careful about it today. I'll tell you each time I don't hear it when you speak.' Even with young learners, it is worth explaining the meaning of fluency and accuracy and the value of each in the overall learning of a language.

Using appropriate language

What steps can you take to ensure that you use appropriate language for students at different levels?

It is possible to identify the language which will be used regularly in your classes. There are a number of expressions which you are likely to use frequently. Some of these you will want your students to use, both when they speak to you and when they speak to each other. Consider, for example, the expressions which are needed for polite exchanges. Decide which ones you are likely to use yourself and which you will teach your students so that they can use them. In a beginners' class, for example, you may wish to teach everyone to say such things as:

–Excuse me.
–I'm sorry.
–Thank you.
–Good morning/afternoon/etc.
–I don't understand.
–Have you got . . .
–Please pass me . . .
–I can't see the picture/the board/etc.
–Whose is this?
–Be careful!

You can teach these expressions very early, simply as formulae, without going into the detail of their grammatical structures, so that they can be used immediately. At first, you will probably need to prompt your students to use them, so that they will become a part of the polite behaviour which you expect in your classes.

You will then need a set of expressions which you will use to deal with the work of the class and which the students will need to understand. There is obviously no point in saying to a student in a beginners' class 'I would never have expected you to have done it so well.' Perhaps you will use such things as:

–Please get out your books.
–Turn to page . . .
–Listen carefully.
–Look at the picture/this word/etc.
–Please repeat . . .
–Well done!
–Good!
–Please don't interrupt.

You usually know when your students are failing to understand you, but they need to learn how to interrupt you and seek help. Then 'Excuse me, Mr . . . , I don't understand' will mean that you must rephrase what you have said or repeat it carefully. It is important not to make students look foolish. Interruptions must be treated seriously so that your students will not be discouraged from seeking help when they need it.

You will enhance the feeling of 'security' in your class if you use the same expressions regularly, adding to the range gradually over time. The way of deciding what to add to your repertoire of teacher language is to include new structures/functions as you come to them in the class coursebook. For example, when you come to the unit which includes *should/would*, you might begin to use 'Would you please close the door, Ruben?' rather than simply 'Please close the door, Ruben,' and when you teach *anybody, somebody, nobody* you might introduce 'Has anybody seen my pen?' rather than 'Where's my pen?'

Giving encouragement

Every opportunity should be taken to give encouragement to students who are making a real effort and not just to those who are being most successful. This can be done briefly and frequently, without interrupting the flow of the lesson, by the use of 'Yes', 'Good', 'That's right' and even by a simple nod of the head. In addition, a comment, however brief, on written work is much more encouraging than just a mark.

Clearly you will want to avoid comparing one student's performance with that of other students. Such things as 'Well done, Lee. I don't know why the rest of you can't do as well as Lee' and 'Can't you ever get anything right? I've never seen work as bad as this' are unlikely to improve the performance of those who are being criticised. Comparing a student's work with his or her own previous performance is more constructive and gives the student a sense of how he or she is progressing. Such things as 'That's better, Ramon, well done,' or 'You are still having problems with your spelling, Ramon, you must take care,' are likely to show Ramon that you are genuinely interested in his work, and that you are not merely measuring him against the others.

Involving all the students

How can a teacher ensure that all the students are included in oral practice?

In large classes in particular, it is very easy to miss some students out when doing oral practice. Teachers need ways of ensuring that every student gets a fair share of turns at asking or responding or whatever, without all the rest of the class losing interest.

You will often wish to get just one student to reply to a question or respond to a statement. If you say 'Eva, where shall I put this picture?', all the other students will 'switch off' as soon as you say 'Eva'. A useful technique for a teacher is, therefore, to ask the question–'Where shall I put this picture?'–pause for a second, and then add 'Eva'. (Teaching is probably the only situation in which this format is used at all regularly.) If you practise doing this with all your classes for a couple of weeks, it will become second nature to you.

Many teachers tend to focus on one particular section of the class, although they do not realise it. It may be the area where the very good students sit, it may be the front, or the area by the window. Consider whether you have this tendency. Simply recognising it will help you to adjust your focus and spread your attention more generally around the class.

Here are some ways of endeavouring to include all the students:

1 Use the class register list. Obviously the students will know if you are calling on them in the order of the list, but if you use every second or third name, or some other pattern, they may not realise what order you are using. This method has the disadvantage that you will tend to look down at the list, which is not a very natural way to address somebody, so you need to have the list where you can see it easily. Some teachers write all the names on a strip of paper which they then use as a bookmark for their coursebook. To prevent students who have just responded from 'switching off' when they've had their turn, it's a good idea to ask one or two for a second response later in the sequence.

2 Think of your class as a set of lines or rows of students and address a question to a person from each line/row in turn.

3 If you have a few students who tend to shout out the answers before anybody else has time to try, make a rule on some occasions that when a student has responded once he or she must miss the next three chances and can then answer again. This gives the one who must remain silent something to do (i.e. count) and the knowledge that he or she can soon join in again; it is better than saying to a student 'Ude, don't answer any more.'

4 After you have asked the first question, invite the one who answers to name the person who will answer the next one. If your students get used to this system, it can move quite briskly and be very successful. However, it can become unpleasant if the students see it as a way of victimising fellow students. If this seems to be the case with a particular group, it's better not to use it again.

5 If the student you ask is unable to respond you will nearly always want to assist him or her by repeating or prompting, and will have to insist that the rest of the class remains quiet. Sometimes, however, you may wish to pass the question to another student, or the class in general, especially if it is a factual question–'When will the festival begin, Henri?' When it is clear that Henri is not able to reply, you could ask 'When will the festival begin? Do you know, Florence?' and, if Florence cannot answer, 'When will the festival begin? Who knows?' Then you can select one from those who put up their hands, although it may be that someone will shout out the answer and you can then reinforce it with 'Yes, it will begin on 14th March. That's right.' Avoid asking 'Can anybody help Henri?' (see page 36).

Teachers are often advised to rephrase their statements and questions if their students are having difficulty in understanding, but this has to be done with great care. It is often the case that the rephrasing produces a more complex utterance than the original one. Take the question: 'When will the festival begin?' If a student appears not to have understood or has not paid attention, the teacher might say: 'I said, "When will the festival begin?"', thus adding something to what has already not been grasped. Or the teacher might say 'Henri, I asked you when the festival would begin,' creating yet greater difficulty. You need to be aware of this, so that you can take care when rephrasing to produce an utterance which will assist the learner. It's often possible simply to repeat the utterance, stressing the part which has apparently caused the difficulty. For example: 'What did the man say, Yoshiko?' 'He went out of the room, Miss Jackson.' 'Yes, but what did the man *say*?', thus indicating to Yoshiko where she has gone wrong. (One of the great advantages of recorded material is that utterances can be played over and over again and the structure, stress and intonation will be identical every time.)

The place of examinations and tests

How can you help your students face examinations and tests with confidence, so that the atmosphere of the class is not spoiled by them?

Only a small proportion of language learners study without the prospect of examinations at the end of their course, or even within their course. It is easy to allow an exam to dominate the work and to use it as a kind of justification, or even threat. Whilst examinations are, of course, very important, teachers must help students to keep them in proper perspective.

What can be done? It is worthwhile talking to your students about the examinations they will take. You can explain which exams they will be entered for and when they will occur. You can describe the form of the exams, the kinds of question to expect, the things the examiners will be looking for. You should tell the class how the work that they will do with you will help them to prepare for their exams. They will then feel confident that you know that the syllabus is relevant to their needs. Clearly, many class activities will not seem of immediate relevance, but your students will be happy to participate if they know that the overall scheme is moving them towards their goal.

As the day of the exam approaches, your students' level of anxiety may rise and they will ask more and more questions about the exam. It's important to answer these questions and to give the students any information they need. Some practice in doing exam-type exercises, perhaps timed test questions, will be helpful too.

If you are in the habit of using tests in class to check progress fairly regularly, it is important for your students to know that this is your purpose, so that the tests do not become like mini-exams where scores are the overriding concern. You can reduce the tension when giving class tests by asking the students to mark their own papers, or by arranging for them to exchange with a neighbour; by discussing the answers as you give them and by not giving too much weight to the marks scored. Marking in class also has the advantage of the students getting immediate feedback.

Another way of lowering the tension caused by tests in class, and of encouraging collaboration, is to invite your students to compare their answers with others in pairs or groups once they have completed the test and to decide what they think are the right answers before you provide any solutions.

Extra-curricular activities

Extra activities, conducted outside lesson times, can make a significant contribution to maintaining a good atmosphere in the classroom. If a greater command of English is seen to open the way to interesting activities, your students will take a more positive attitude to their studies. By organising a class library or an English club you can provide your students with the possibility of extending their knowledge and interests outside the classroom as well as giving them an opportunity for genuine communication. It is clearly best if you can help set these things up and then get students to run them with whatever assistance they need from you. If the school runs an English club, the students are further advantaged by mixing with and talking to students at other levels and either being able to assist younger students or to learn from older ones.

The important thing is to provide situations where English can be the natural language for what is being done. Such things as film or video shows, play-readings, food preparation, holiday planning and so on can form the basis of activities which students at all levels and stages of learning can enjoy.

This chapter has put forward a variety of suggestions for establishing and maintaining a purposeful, happy class atmosphere. You may have already marked ideas that you think you might adopt. Why not look through the chapter again quickly and select some strategies which you will try? Write them into the chart on page 45 and use it as your checklist for action.

An encouraging class atmosphere

Three things I'll do to achieve a happy, purposeful atmosphere in my classes	1 _____ 2 _____ 3 _____
Five polite phrases which I'll expect the students in Class . . . . . . to use regularly	1 _____ 2 _____ 3 _____ 4 _____ 5 _____
Five phrases of encouragement which I'll use with Class	1 _____ 2 _____ 3 _____ 4 _____ 5 _____
Two ways in which I'll try to involve all the students in oral practice	1 _____ 2 _____
One thing that I'll never do again!	_____ _____

The classroom itself

This chapter is all about the physical conditions in which you and your students work in the classroom:

- the lightness/brightness
- the temperature and fresh air
- the acoustics
- the lines of vision
- the layout of the desks/tables
- the possibility of moving desks/tables
- the other furniture
- the facilities for displaying pictures, charts, etc.

The chapter concludes with some suggestions for taking advantage of the communicative language possibilities related to the physical conditions of the classroom.

In considering each of the sections in this chapter, it is important to relate the suggestions to your own particular situation. The degree of freedom to make changes to the teaching environment varies from school to school and from country to country. It may be, however, that changes have not been made in the past in your school because nobody has proposed them.

You will be very fortunate if you have been able to choose which classroom you use for your classes. Most teachers have to accept the room(s) they are allocated for their work. Indeed, many are required to teach in a variety of rooms each day as groups of students remain in 'their' rooms and teachers move from one class to another. English teachers might sometimes envy the teachers of physics or biology or chemistry who have areas set aside for their subjects where they can leave apparatus, charts, etc. and where students find a kind of 'focal point' for those subjects.

In schools and colleges where there are fixed rooms for English, teachers have the opportunity to create an appropriate environment (with wall-charts, posters and the like) so that everyone coming into one of those rooms knows immediately that here English is the focus of attention. But teachers who must move from class to class can also do quite a lot to ensure that the environment in which their classes are held is as encouraging as possible.

Consider one of *your* teaching rooms:

1 *Is the room light and bright (but not too bright)?*

Do you remember sitting in a class in a dull room when you were a student? If you do, you'll probably recollect that it was harder to be enthusiastic about lessons in that room (unless the teacher was especially good) than it was in lighter, brighter rooms.

What can you do about it?

Perhaps you can get brighter lights, move any pictures that are on the windows, move the furniture to make the best use of what light there is, or even arrange to use another room.

Of course, your problem might be that the room is *too* bright – because the sun glares through the windows making everyone hot and uncomfortable. In this case you might ask for blinds, put pictures on some of the windows, move the furniture to move students out of the direct sunlight, or arrange to use another room.

2 *Is the temperature comfortable and the air fresh?*

If a classroom is used continuously throughout the day, it will get very stuffy and unpleasant to be in, unless someone ensures that fresh air is introduced. So can you do anything to improve the temperature and the freshness of the air?

It's worth getting into the habit of checking when you go into a classroom whether you need to have any windows opened, any blinds pulled down to block off the heat from the sun, even the door left open to produce a through draught on a very hot day, the air-conditioning/heating turned on/off, up/down, etc.

You will also want to check sometimes if the window being open or the air-conditioning being turned up is causing discomfort. You can ask your students to say if they are not comfortable.

3 *Is it easy for everyone to hear you?*

Unfortunately, many schools are built of materials chosen for their strength and durability, rather than their acoustic properties. Teachers frequently have to teach in rooms in which it is difficult to hear and be heard. This is very tiring for everyone concerned, and there are only a limited number of things you can do about it.

Try to decide whether each of your teaching rooms has particular acoustic features and then adjust your voice to suit the conditions.

Concrete walls and high smooth ceilings generally cause a lot of echoes. In these rooms, lowering your voice to the level at which you don't 'boom', but making sure that everyone can still hear, is often helpful. (The same adjustment will apply to the sound level of a cassette recorder – see page 83.)

Carpets, curtains, cushions and the like absorb sound, and so in a room with a lot of soft furnishings you may need to compensate – this time by raising your voice a little.

Open windows let in noises from outside (and many closed windows do too!), so you may need to compromise between your desire for fresh air and the need for you and your students to be able to hear one another clearly. One possibility is to close the windows during those parts of the lesson when hearing clearly across the room is important and to open them when, for example, the students are doing pair or group work.

4 *Can all the students see you and the board or screen easily?*

Obviously you don't stand in one spot and you don't want your students to look at the board all the time, but it's important for them to be able to see clearly without having to strain to do so.

What can you do about it?

Why not:

- check whether everyone can see at least your face and your hands (because you want them to see any gestures you make). The easiest way to check is simply to ask your students. Move from place to place in the room and ask 'Can you see me clearly when I stand here? Can you see my hands?' You'll probably find that there are just one or two places where you are most easily seen by everyone. While you can, of course, speak to the class from any part of the room, it's probably helpful to go to one of these spots if you have any particularly important point to make to the class in general.

- point out to your students that they should tell you if they are unable to see you clearly when they need to, so that you can move into a better position to help them.

Poor lines of vision

- avoid making a habit of standing with your back to the window, as you will only be seen as a silhouette and students will not have the benefit of seeing your facial expression to help them understand what you say.

- check that the board/overhead projector screen is clearly visible to everyone, again by asking. If you have a fixed board, you may find that some parts of it are more easily seen than others (because of the light or the height), so get into the habit of avoiding the 'bad' patches.

5 *Are you free to change the layout of the classroom?*

It may be that, in your school, moving any classroom furniture is out of the question. This doesn't mean that you are precluded from organising pair work or group work or even role play. All of these activities can be carried out in almost any surroundings, and their value is so great that it is worth putting up with any inconvenience they cause.

As a rule, moving people around is much easier than moving desks! Indeed, the informality which results from having to form pairs or groups without shifting desks and tables can be a positive advantage in motivating your students and getting them to communicate with each other. Pair work rarely requires more than turning round or moving along and can therefore be done frequently and briefly with-

Pair work

out fuss. Even for group work it is often just not worth the effort of moving all the furniture around, although re-positioning a few chairs is often helpful. However, you may be tempted to reorganise the seating quite drastically, perhaps for a particular lesson or series of lessons, or even for the whole course. If you are teaching in a room which lots of other teachers use for other subjects, then you have to be careful not to leave the desks in an order that they don't like.

What can you do about it?

You can, perhaps:

- talk to the other users of a particular room and ask whether they would like the desks arranged differently. You may (perhaps!) find that all the teachers would prefer another layout.

- decide whether two or three minutes used at the beginning and end of each lesson to move the desks or chairs for your purposes is worthwhile in the interests of providing a better environment.

- reconsider whether you can achieve the same results without altering the layout. Can you manage to form pairs or groups just by asking your students to turn round in their seats, to sit on desks (if it's not forbidden in your school!), or to 'squash up' a bit? It's sometimes possible to make things easier by putting one group round the teacher's desk, so that other groups have room to move.

6 *How can you organise the moving of the furniture? Which layouts work well?*

To avoid the chaos of having everyone trying to help, it's a good idea to ask a small number of people to move the furniture before everyone else comes into the room, if that's possible. And, of course, don't forget to have it all moved back again at the end of the lesson.

If you wish to move some furniture *during* a lesson, ask individuals by name to help by moving this or that.

If you are a regular furniture mover, you will probably discover that there are just two or three layouts that you will use. The patterns will of course vary according to the size and shape of the room.

POSSIBLE LAYOUTS

Pattern 1 Good for group work

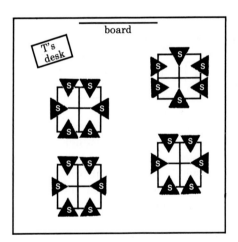

Pattern 1 is particularly good for group work. It gives students a sense of belonging to a particular group as they all face in towards each other. Any papers or books that they all need to use can be put in the centre of the group. Anyone who is going to write (notes for the group response, for example) can do so without losing touch with the rest of the group. Almost any class activity can be carried out in this pattern, although it is annoying for students who have to turn round every time they need to look at the board.

Using pattern 1 gives a lot of opportunity for interaction between students. The teacher needs to ensure that tasks are clearly explained and students know whether they are to work alone or in pairs or groups. For teachers who are used to a more formal arrangement—with the teacher facing rows of students—it is advisable to try out this less formal pattern with one or two specific tasks, and reflect on its advantages and disadvantages before making it a regularly used layout.

Pattern 2 Good for role play, simulations, etc.

Pattern 2 focuses attention towards the front of the class, though not necessarily towards the teacher. It has the advantage that most students can see each other's faces and so are more likely to pay attention to what others say. It provides a setting for any 'front of class' activities. Pair work can be done perfectly well with this kind of layout as the students can simply turn to face their partner without moving any furniture.

Pattern 3 allows face-to-face discussion between partners, and means that all students can see the board by simply turning to the front. In a full classroom it can be awkward for the teacher to move around the room with this layout.

Pattern 3 Good for pair work

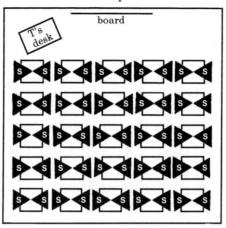

7 *What about the other furniture in the room? A teacher's desk? Storage units? Somewhere to stand equipment when you need to use it?*

Many schools have teacher's desks or tables which are very big and difficult (if not impossible) to move. And many classrooms have nowhere for teachers or students to lay things out, either to use them or to store them.

There is only one thing to do if you have a huge, heavy, immovable teacher's desk and that is *not* to spend your time behind it. It is much harder to communicate with your students from behind a big desk and it certainly discourages them from looking on you as their friend and helper. So you will need to come out from behind your barrier to become part of the group. You might simply stand beside/in front of your desk, perch on the front edge of the desk if you want to rest a bit, bring your chair out from behind the desk (or use another chair), or move around to various parts of the class. By holding your book or papers in your hand, you make your face more visible than when you look down at a book on your desk, and this is a help to your students too (as well as making it easier for you to see what they are doing!).

Storage is another matter for consideration by teachers. There may be problems associated with storing materials in classrooms in your school: they may get lost or spoilt, or it may be against school policy. If you do have secure storage units, you will be able to leave materials (and perhaps equipment) ready for use. You may decide to allocate parts of the storage space for specific items–self-access materials, students' projects, pictures, tapes, etc.–and you could label the shelves to make finding things easier for yourself, your students and, perhaps, other teachers and students who may use the items. If you can't use or don't have storage facilities in your teaching room, you will need to devise a way of organising the many things you need so that you can find them easily and bring them to the classroom. Labelled boxes can prove invaluable to a teacher who has lots of things to store. Large envelopes or folders (also labelled) are useful too. Loose piles of papers tend to get mixed up, particularly if more than one person has access to them. Whatever the method you adopt, you should try to ensure that you can find what you want when you want it with the minimum of trouble.

Most teachers now use cassette recorders rather than open-reel tape recorders in their classes, and so the area needed to put them on while in use is somewhat smaller. The teacher's desk is not always the best place to stand the machine, particularly if it is some way from the students. You may have a small table or a spare desk which you can position closer to the class and on which you can then stand the cassette recorder. Teachers quite often put their equipment on one of the students' desks near the front of the class. Some students find this irritating (and almost certainly too loud), and so you should always ask the student first, and avoid taking over the same desk every time. You can sometimes ask a student to operate the machine for you, but be careful then that it is placed in such a way that others can hear clearly. You will need to experiment to find precisely where to place the cassette recorder, or video recorder if you have one, so that all the students can hear, and for video see as well.

It is often the length of a lead which determines where a piece of equipment is placed, but this should not be so. If extension leads are available in your school, make use of them to improve your choice of location for any equipment you need. If you do use an extension lead, or any long lead, you must be careful to avoid having it trailing across the floor where it may cause an accident. Try to run it round the edge of the room (not across the doorway). If it must cross the room, put a chair over it in the place where people might otherwise trip on it.

8 *Can you stick pictures, notices, etc. on the walls? Is there a notice-board available for you to use?*

The amount of material which is stuck on walls often seems to be determined by some general school policy. But it may not be so. It may simply be that no one else has wished to stick up pictures or charts, or that some teachers like pictures whilst others don't.

So what can you do about it?

Be sure you know of any school policy. Ask your Head of Department or Principal if necessary. Check whether sticking things on windows, gloss-painted doors, etc. is acceptable. Ask if you can stick things up provided you don't leave marks on the wall (and then make sure you use an adhesive material that doesn't mark!).

You may find that your classroom has a notice-board which you can use. If you can't stick things all over it, you might be able to negotiate to have an 'English corner' on the board. If you do that, or indeed if you use the whole notice-board, you must be careful not to leave it covered with out-of-date, dog-eared pieces of paper.

If you move round from classroom to classroom, you might decide to ask for an English notice-board in a corridor. You should then be sure that it's as informative and attractive as possible, so that everyone in the school will want to see what's posted up there. If you can choose the location of your notice-board, select a well-lit position, not too close to a door.

Exploiting opportunities for communicative language use

The organisation of the classroom itself provides opportunities for using English as the language of communication in a very immediate and real situation. From the very beginning, it is best to give instructions and to ask your students to help in English, using gestures to help them understand. At first you will probably use the imperative 'Open the big window' rather than 'Would you mind opening the big window', but you can make it into a polite request by adding 'please' and generally addressing someone by name – 'Open the big window please, Ingrid,' so that your students get used to the type of language that is used in the outside world. If your request has not been completely understood or if the student is obviously hesitant, you can help by making an encouraging remark – 'That's right. Good. The big window.' And when the task has been completed, do remember to say 'Thank you' and add a word or two to confirm that the right thing has been done (i.e. that the request has been understood).

In time, you may decide to give responsibility for organising the classroom to one of your students. You might put a different person in charge for each lesson. This gives individuals the opportunity to give instructions and make requests and gives the rest of the class the opportunity to follow instructions given by someone other than the teacher. Perhaps you could make it a rule that the person in charge doesn't carry out any of the tasks him or herself but must ask other class members to do them. A list of dates of lessons and names could be put on the notice-board (even making the list could form a topic for group work). You will also need a list of things the person in charge has to check: for example, the board and board cleaner, the air-conditioner/heater, the windows, the layout of the desks, the connecting up of any equipment, the tidiness of the notice-board.

By the time you get to asking students to be in charge, they will be familiar with some of the forms for giving instructions and making requests which you have been using regularly in the class. They might use such expressions as:

–Open the window, please.
–Can you close the door, please?
–Would you move that table, please?
–Could you switch on the lights, please?
–Would you help Maria move the board, please?

They will also know how to make courteous responses when something has been done:

–Thank you.
–That's right. Good!
–Fine!

The person in charge can start organising the room as soon as the students begin to arrive, or immediately after the last lesson has finished. It should only occupy a few minutes (maybe less than a minute) as the class settles down.

Most students like being asked to help and happily accept responsibility for particular tasks. The teacher of English should exploit every opportunity to seek assistance as this is one of the limited number of chances for genuine communicative language use which occurs in the classroom. The general rule should be 'Never do anything yourself that you can ask your students to do'!

It's very easy to get used to an unsatisfactory environment and to fail even to make the changes which can be made with little or no trouble. So, before leaving this chapter, complete the checklist below for the room you use most frequently. Having decided what action (if any) to take, try to do something about it within the next couple of weeks.

Features to consider	Present conditions	Action that I will take
Lightness/brightness		
Temperature and fresh air		
Acoustics		
Lines of vision		
Layout of desks/tables		
Possibility of moving desks/tables		
Ancillary furniture		
Facilities for displaying pictures, charts, etc.		

Be prepared

In this chapter, you will find ways of deciding what work to do with your various classes and suggestions for making lesson plans so that you can always be in control of your students' learning programme. The chapter also considers how a teacher can vary the amount of work covered in a particular lesson depending on the time available and on the progress of the class. Finally, a few ideas are given on how to cope with emergencies.

A scheme of work

A scheme of work is a kind of 'map' of the work that is to be done and when it should be done. You may have an overall target for the year which is broken down into sections. Local practice varies. In some countries, the ministry or department of education requires that schemes of work are prepared and submitted for scrutiny and

<table>
<tr><td colspan="4" rowspan="2"></td><td>Year</td><td>2</td></tr>
<tr><td>Class</td><td>2c</td></tr>
<tr><td colspan="4" rowspan="2">CENTRAL SCHOOL
DEPARTMENT OF ENGLISH
SCHEME OF WORK</td><td>Term</td><td>1</td></tr>
<tr><td>Coursebook</td><td>Focus</td></tr>
<tr><td>Week</td><td>Course-book unit</td><td>Functions</td><td>Language structures</td><td>Topic/situation</td><td>Possible additional activities</td></tr>
<tr><td>9</td><td>7</td><td>Asking for and giving directions, politely</td><td>Can you tell me the way to ..., please?
How do I get to.... please?

Go up/down/along...
Walk up/down/along...
If you go...</td><td>In the street</td><td>-Listening to recorded instructions and following the route on map

-Drill – using flash cards

-Pair work – using map</td></tr>
<tr><td>10</td><td>11</td><td>Making a request and responding to a request, politely</td><td>Will you please...
Would you please...
Would you mind....ing, please</td><td>A patient in a hospital bed is being visited by a friend (use before course-book unit, as intro)</td><td>Listening to a recorded conversation drill

-Substitution drill

-Role play</td></tr>
</table>

agreement every year, term, or month – even every fortnight or week. In others, schemes of work are agreed centrally and teachers in all the schools follow the pattern laid down. You need, of course, to know what the practice is where you work. Whether you prepare your own or whether you use one prepared by somebody else, it is important to have a scheme to follow. The longer the period which your scheme covers, the more flexible it must be. You need to have achievable targets, but also to be ready to adjust them if necessary.

If you work in a situation where schemes of work are not imposed from outside the school, you have a number of ways of establishing what your scheme will be. Here are three possible sources:

1 The English department or the senior English teacher may have drawn up a programme for each of the levels in the school. If so, you are probably expected to follow this pattern. Upon close examination, it may show, for example, a sequence in which verb forms of increasing difficulty are to be introduced. If it is a well-thought-out scheme, it will incorporate opportunities for revision of what has already been learned.

2 If no such agreed school scheme exists, you may simply be told which coursebook you must use for a particular level. A careful look at the contents page of such a book will, if it is a reasonably well-planned book, reveal a progression and built-in revision. By using the contents list as a guide, and looking at the actual units, you will be able to break down the work into lessons.

3 Examination boards normally produce a syllabus upon which the examination is based. This syllabus, or perhaps only a part of it, can be used as a basis for drawing up a scheme of work. In this case, you will probably have to decide for yourself the order in which the various items should be introduced. You will also need to plan for some revision of parts already covered.

If none of these sources is immediately available to you, you will need to provide a scheme of work for yourself. To achieve this, it is almost certainly simplest to examine all the coursebooks at about the right level which are available and then, if you are free to make the choice, base your work on the units of one of the books. You do, of course, need to consult the other English teachers in the school. You won't want to repeat work the students have already covered in a previous year, nor to do work which in your colleagues' view should be held back for later years.

As well as deciding on the actual content of your teaching and the order in which to tackle each thing, you will want to give some thought to *how* you are going to teach. You may have been told that you must use the language laboratory every Wednesday, or that your class never uses the language laboratory, and so you need to plan with all such restrictions in mind. Obviously you can't plan every lesson in detail before the course begins, as what you do from week to week is influenced by how things have gone in previous lessons. You do, however, need to know in advance whether you will be the only English teacher taking a class and, if not, how the work will be shared. Will you, for example, do mainly oral work, leaving a colleague to do most of the written work? Will you work through the coursebook, simply going on from where your colleague stopped at the end of the last lesson? Will someone else be teaching 'Literature', and overlapping with what you are doing in your lessons? Will 'assistants' be conducting some lessons, or taking groups out of your lessons for conversation practice? Who will set the end-of-year examination? Will this influence what parts of the syllabus each of you teaches? Clearly, it is more difficult to organise a class which is shared than to be the class's only English teacher. But it can also be rewarding and helpful to have a colleague with whom you can discuss the students' progress in detail and to whom you can turn if you feel there are problems to be solved.

Having a fairly firm idea of what the overall scheme for the term or the year is going to be makes the planning of individual lessons much easier and speedier. Time invested at the beginning of the academic year, preferably before teaching starts, pays dividends throughout the year when you are busy with day-to-day teaching and other duties.

However you plan your work you will want to be satisfied that you give your students a varied diet of activities. A good balance would include controlled oral practice, oral fluency work, reading comprehension, listening comprehension, and written work of all sorts. All or any of these activities provide opportunities for pair work or group work, for projects or problem solving.

You might find it useful to draw up a 'timetable' for each class which breaks down the English lessons into various kinds of activity, so that you can be sure that you do not neglect any important areas. Depending on how frequently you teach a class, you could plan a weekly or a fortnightly timetable along these lines:

Class **4A** Room **12** **(Wed: Language lab)**		
Monday 10–11 Presentation of new items Coursebook work Reading comprehension Collect homework	**Wednesday 9–10** Oral drills/oral fluency work Listening comprehension Return homework	**Friday 14–15** Revision of items introduced this week and last week Coursebook work Set homework

Lesson plans

Trainee teachers spend a lot of time preparing very detailed plans. With experience, doing this planning becomes quicker, but it never ceases to be an important part of a teacher's job. It is not only inefficient, but it is unprofessional to go to a lesson without having given proper consideration to what you are going to do in that lesson.

In some parts of the world, teachers are required to make lesson plans according to an officially laid down format. You may, for example, have a book of lesson preparation forms which you must complete and have available to show those in authority when required. You may have been told to lay out your lesson plans in a way which is used by everyone in your school or your department.

Inexperienced teachers find that a carefully prepared lesson plan is a great help when they are in the class. The plan should not be too long and complicated as the teacher can only take quick glances at it during the lesson. In fact, some teachers do make detailed lesson notes and then, either on the side of the notes (perhaps in another colour) or on a separate sheet of paper, make an outline plan, which is the part looked at during the lesson. Examples of lesson plans are shown on pages 62–64.

Lesson Plan

Class: Date and time:

Aims:

New lexis:

Equipment:

Material:

Before the class:

(Timing) | Method:

Homework to set:

Comment on lesson:

Lesson Plan

Class:

Room No:

Date:

Time: Length of lesson:

Aims:

- functional

- structural

- phonological

- skills

Materials:

Aids:

Homework:

Evaluation of procedure:

64

Lesson Plan

Class: Date: Time:

Overall aim:

Activity	Material and aids	Time needed	Skills to be practised	Problems anticipated

Homework:

How the lesson went:

There is no one absolutely right way to draw up a plan and each teacher will decide what suits him or her best. Time can be saved, however, by deciding on a format which suits you and then keeping a pile of blanks. Then you always produce your plans on a sheet which looks exactly the same and you get used to glancing at the right part of the paper during the lesson.

It is a good idea not to throw away your lesson plans, but to keep them in a folder or loose-leaf file (perhaps one for each class you teach). In this way, you can consider whether to use them again in future years, modified as necessary. The advantage of the loose-leaf system is that you can replace plans which did not work well, or change the order if you want to.

Writing a comment after each lesson is a useful habit for a teacher to get into. It is easy, in the haste to get to the next class, for the lesson just given to be forgotten. The kind of comment which will prove helpful to you might be 'too much new vocabulary, insufficient time for oral drills'; 'picture too small, must not use again'; 'students particularly liked the story on page 28 of coursebook, led to good discussion'; 'material boring'; 'could have used more pair work for oral practice stage'; 're-do'.

A copy of any printed material which you have produced for a lesson can be kept with the lesson plan, so that you can consider its relevance for future lessons. If you use other audio-visual aids, you will want to include precise information on your lesson plan about where the material can be found when you need it again. It is extremely frustrating to remember that you used this or that picture/tape/chart to teach the Simple Past to Form 2 last year, and the lesson was a great success, and then not to remember where you got the picture/tape/chart from!

Before leaving this section, why not prepare a lesson-planning format which you think will suit you? Try it out for a few lessons and then change it if you find it's not quite right. As you prepare your format, you will need to provide spaces for:

- details of the class, date etc;
- the aim and/or objectives (i.e. what the students will be able to do by the end of the lesson–for example to be able to ask polite questions using 'May I . . . ?' 'Can I . . . please?');
- the material and aids to be used;
- the stages of the lesson;

- the teacher's comments on the lesson.

Within each of the above stages, you will need to leave room to indicate:

- what precise language will be learned/practised – e.g. the Past Simple form: *turned*, *followed*, *listened*;
- which part of the coursebook – e.g. page 21 exercise 4; and/or what audio-visual aid will be used – e.g. street scene picture;
- whether the students will be reading, writing, speaking or listening;
- how much time to give to each stage.

You will also want a space in which to note what homework you are going to give.

You may think that one of the examples shown on pages 62–64 suits you perfectly well. If so, try it for a few lessons and then consider whether you need to amend it. It could become your way of doing things for the next thirty or forty years, so it's worth investing a few hours on it now!

Timing

One aspect of planning a lesson which sometimes causes difficulty is the question of how much can be done in one lesson. Trainee teachers are generally required to indicate on their plans how much time will be devoted to each activity. With practice, a teacher becomes better able to judge how much time will be needed for each thing. It is worth persevering with writing down an estimate of the time even if, in the event, you find that a particular stage of your lesson takes much longer or much less time than you had anticipated. You may need to omit some stages of your lesson if, for example, an earlier stage takes longer than expected or if there is an unexpected delay or interruption to your class. You will then need to decide whether the stages omitted should be incorporated in a later lesson. You may, on the other hand, find yourself with time to spare, and it is a good idea to have one or two 'reserve' activities which you can use if this occurs. A new teacher might find this more disconcerting than being pressed for time, so here are a few ideas for 'reserve' activities:

- finding all the things in the room beginning with a certain letter of the alphabet;
- singing a song (if this is one of your talents – see page 9);
- telling the students a *very* short story (you need to know a few);
- playing a language game (you could look at some of the ideas in *Techniques for Classroom Interaction* Longman 1987);
- asking the students to solve a puzzle (if you know or can find some);
- revising something learned by the class in a previous lesson.

With experience, teachers learn how to vary the amount of time given to any particular stage of their lessons. Then it's possible, if you so wish, to cover the planned work in the time available, even though you realise that you have planned too little or too much.

Here are some devices for cutting the amount of time taken on various activities:

- Seek fewer individual responses from students; substitute a little more choral practice.
- If group work is planned and groups are to report back, increase the size of each group a little so that there are one or two fewer groups and hence less time is needed for reporting back.
- Postpone any planned written work and set it for homework.
- If you know you will be hard pressed for time, make the first stage (review/warm-up) very short and brisk.
- Miss out some examples of a structure/function.

You may want devices for extending activities. Here are two possibilities:

- Increase the amount of individual response practice (but not by too much because it can be boring for the other students).
- Introduce pair work after you have practised a structure with the class (but you need to be careful that you know precisely what the students *can* practise in pairs).

It is, however, not generally a good policy to try to extend activities by coming up with ideas on the spot, as you will risk both getting things wrong and boring the class. It is almost always better to go on through the planned work and then add an extra activity at the end. If it is the day on which you normally give homework, a popular strategy for using up time is to set the homework and invite the class to start doing it! In fact, this also gives you an opportunity to check that the students are going to be able to do the homework you have set.

Emergencies

Occasionally, you will be asked to take a class for an absent colleague. You may be lucky enough to find that your colleague has already prepared a lesson plan which you can use, or has kept a good record of the work done in previous lessons, so you at least have an indication of what part of the book the class has reached. If you then have time for a bit of planning of your own, you can prepare a good lesson. If, however, you are asked as you are going into a lesson at 10.00 a.m. to take a class at 11.00 a.m., you will need to have an 'emergency' strategy ready. Here are a few ideas to help you cope:

- Ask the students to tell you what they did in the last lesson and go on from that point in the coursebook, doing the best you can.
- Start with a short dictation based on the last lesson the class did. This gives the students the opportunity to get used to your voice and gives you an impression (but only an impression) of how good their English is.
- Take something with which you are familiar from your Resources Box (see pages 90–91). If you can, use this material as the basis for practice of the functions or structures which the class has been studying.
- Get an audio tape or a video tape which you are familiar with and use that as the basis for a lesson (but this depends on the immediate accessibility of the equipment and the material).
- Tell the students that you are going to give them a revision test. You then ask every student to produce a question, not showing it to the others. The questions should be about things learned by the class in previous lessons. Of course, the students can refer to their coursebooks for ideas. Having collected all the questions, you ask the whole class the questions and they write down the answers. Marking can be done by exchanging papers. The one who set the question is asked to provide the correct answer.
- With a more advanced class a decision-making activity/game can be introduced.

You probably have lots more ideas. Why not tick the ideas above which you think you could use and add others to the list now – before your first emergency arises? Then, when you are asked to substitute for a colleague and you don't know what to do, you can just take a quick look at your list and your problem will be solved.

Lesson routines

When you teach a new group of students for the first time, they will be trying to find out all about you and how you behave. First impressions *are* important. Your life will be made easier and your classes more successful if you establish a pattern in your lessons which everybody understands and accepts, and this is the subject of this chapter.

Attention is focused first on general patterns of behaviour. Then suggestions are made for managing the various operational steps in a lesson: the beginning, changes of activity, arranging of students into pairs and groups, and the end of the lesson.

General classroom behaviour

There are almost certainly some patterns of behaviour which are general to your school. Perhaps all students are expected to stand when the teacher comes into the room, perhaps they are expected to sit in their places in silence. It may be that homework is collected by a student rather than by a teacher, and that the board is always cleaned by the person sitting nearest to it. A new teacher should find out what is 'normal' in the school (see Chapter 2, *Know your school*) and should, of course, comply with this pattern. If there are no 'norms' then it is wise to establish some of your own. What you decide will depend very much on the culture of the country in which you work, and to some extent on your own cultural background. The pattern you choose should not, of course, include anything which might offend your students, your colleagues or your employers.

Getting the lesson started

It's probably most friendly to allow the students to continue to talk *quietly*, whilst remaining in their seats, until you announce that you are ready to begin the lesson. This prevents you from being under pressure to hurry. It also makes it clear that when you require silence it is so that the work can get under way, rather than 'because you are a teacher'.

'Hands up'

The idea of putting up hands is not always appropriate in a language class because you will sometimes need to seek responses from those who don't know (or who do, but don't put up their hands). Many language teachers ask their students not to put up their hands (but it's hard for them to remember not to if they are in the habit of doing so in all their other lessons). The teacher then asks for responses by naming a student *after* the question has been asked (see page 41), and then sometimes gradually widening the range if the named student is unable to answer (see page 42).

Quite often students are asked to put up their hands before asking a question. This is a convenient device in a large class and helps to prevent lots of noisy interruptions. However, it would be a pity to insist on students always raising their hands before speaking and not to respond immediately to a spontaneous 'Could you repeat that, please, Miss Jackson?' One of the skills of language use which is especially helpful to a language learner is the ability to interrupt and seek clarification. Too strict an insistence on students putting up their hands for this purpose robs them of this particular experience.

It is generally useful to get students to raise their hands to attract your attention if they are working quietly at a written task and want individual help. It's also a good idea when students are carrying out group activities because the level of noise tends to get higher when individuals raise their voices to make themselves heard over the general buzz of several conversations.

If you have not already done so, you could consider now why and when you want your students to put up their hands before speaking. Having decided what you'll do, tell your students what you expect and explain to them why you think your system is the right one.

What to bring to class

Students who move from room to room for different lessons need to know in advance of the lesson what books, or other things, they will need to bring. This means that you have to plan in advance and be sure the students know what they will need. You could tell them at the beginning of the course 'You should always bring your coursebook, your dictionary and your rough notebook' or whatever 'unless I tell you otherwise.' Then you should be firm in reprimanding anyone who fails to bring what is needed to the first few lessons, so that it becomes second nature for your students to bring the right books. On the other hand, if you ask the class to bring a book and for six consecutive lessons you never refer to it, it would be unfair to be cross if someone failed to bring it to the seventh lesson. You can change the list of what is to be brought from time to time. Of course, you need to add items occasionally for particular activities you have planned, e.g. 'Please be sure to have a ruler with you for Friday's lesson. You're all going to need rulers to do some measuring for your project.'

With younger learners it is a good idea to insist that they do not have things on the desk which are not to be used during the lesson. The temptation to do the history homework rather than pay attention to the English lesson can be overwhelming!

Where notes are made

How students use their various notebooks is also worth some forethought. If students buy their own coursebooks there is no reason why they should not write in them, mark things they want to remember, even colour the pictures. For language learning in particular this is one of the advantages of students owning their books. The location of words on the page, the juxtaposition of pictures and words, the odd jotting made during a lesson all help when students wish to remember and use that word or expression again later. If, however, books belong to the school and are, or will be, used by a number of different students, then it is important to establish some other way in which students can make notes, lists, etc. The notes they make need to be easily accessible and readily put in context when needed. Some kind of notebook seems to be an almost essential tool for the language learner. You can make it a more useful tool by helping your students establish an organised way of keeping their notes. The simplest system is probably to use the chapter/unit titles of the coursebook and perhaps the exercise/section/activity number as headings. The students can then write what they wish under these headings and the notebook can be referred to alongside the coursebook. This will perhaps jog the

> **Mysteries and Theories**
>
> to cast a spell on someone
>
> to put a curse on someone
>
> Text = curse → (malediction)
>
>   tomb → a place for a dead body with a monument or something over it.
>
>   remote → far
>
>   foliage → leaves on trees.
>
>   rip → to tear quickly.
>
> Remote = in remote parts of the country.
>
>   to live in a house remote from the nearest village
>
>   he's very remote → he behaves in a distant way.
>
>   to go to the dogs → to be ruined.
>
>   (? slang)

A page from a student's notebook

student's memory about why he or she wrote something down when he or she refers back to the notes at a later date.

Forms of address

If you teach young people in a school (as opposed to older learners in a college), there is almost certainly an established way in which students address their teachers and teachers address their students. There is also likely to be an accepted way in which one teacher refers to another when speaking to students–e.g. 'Signora Rocci is away today,' not 'Paola Rocci is away today.'

With older students in college situations or on special courses for, say, a group of tour operators, you need to establish the form of address you will use to them and how you want them to address you. This depends largely on local custom and expectations. Some adults may want to be addressed formally because they are older than the rest of the group or more senior in their job, or because they feel ill at ease for some reason. You might therefore decide to use a mixture of first names – Lee, Barjit – and family names – Mr Singh, Miss Schmidt – with a particular class. If everybody is happy to do so, it's often convenient for you and easier for fellow students to use first names when addressing members of the class.

Make it clear from the outset what your own name is and how you like to be addressed. In some cultures, there are teaching situations in which the teacher may be called by his or her first name, but in others this is not acceptable. Teachers should take into account not just their own preferences, but also local 'norms' in this matter.

A little time can usefully be spent at the beginning of the course explaining how you intend the class to operate, and making it plain what you consider to be acceptable behaviour. Clearly this should be done in a friendly but firm manner, not sounding threatening and 'teacher-ish'.

Beginning a lesson

A few simple DOs:

1 DO try to arrive with everything you need for the class. Leaving to fetch forgotten items breaks the continuity and gives an opportunity for minds (at the very least!) to wander.

2 DO glance around to see that the room is ready. Are the windows open/shut to suit you? Is the board/overhead projector clean? If not, ask the students to help.

3 DO look around to see where the students are sitting. Does the arrangement suit you? Can you change anything if it doesn't? Can you get close to each student if you want to (to answer a query, to look at work, etc.)? Do you need to ask students to put away things from their desks?

4 DO be sure you are ready before beginning the actual lesson. Arrange your books, papers, etc. so that you can pick them up

easily as you want them. A nervous teacher tends to rush to start. Whilst you cannot spend too long getting organised, the time you take seems shorter to the students than you may think, and some of them can be busy doing things required under 2 and 3 above.

5 DO make a clear and definite start. You may have said 'Hello' or 'Good morning' to various students as you came in, in an informal way. Now you can declare yourself ready by saying clearly and quite loudly 'Good morning, everybody' and waiting for silence (or perhaps a reply of 'Good morning, Mr Black') before going on.

6 DO say briefly what the plan for the lesson is so that the students can be aware of the way they are progressing through the work, e.g. 'Today we're going to learn some more ways of asking to borrow things. We'll be using Unit 12 in our books. And I've brought a basket full of things for you to borrow from me! We'll do some pair work too. But first of all, I want to ask what you all did last night,' (i.e. the first part of the lesson is a review of the Past Simple).

Your way of beginning lessons will soon become known to the students and they may even get on with their part of the preparations without your having to ask. The routine nature of this part of the lesson establishes a secure environment. It sets up an atmosphere which is friendly but purposeful and conducive to serious but enjoyable work.

Changes of activity

During a lesson, you almost always move from one activity to another, perhaps two or three times. You probably also change the pattern of interaction from time to time, so that for some part of the lesson students are working with each other, in pairs or in groups, rather than relating directly to you. There is a wide range of interaction patterns which you can use, including:

- all students listening to the teacher;
- all students listening to recorded material;
- students repeating individually or chorally;
- individual students responding to the teacher;
- reading sections of the coursebook (silently or the teacher reading aloud);
- students making notes (e.g. vocabulary) in notebooks;

- students completing written exercises individually;
- students working in pairs to complete written exercises;
- students doing oral practice in pairs;
- students solving problems in groups;
- students preparing material (stories, questions, etc.) in groups;
- group discussion of a topic;
- students completing tests individually.

The activities you choose will be the ones which suit the objectives you have for the lesson. Many of the activities will be based on material in the coursebook. For all students, but especially for weaker students, a clear indication of a change of activity is motivating, as it gives a new chance to those who have not enjoyed or not done well in the last activity. It is a good idea to say something like: 'Right. We've finished Section Two, so we'll leave our books for today and go on to the story.' Then you should say exactly what you want the students to do for the next activity, e.g. 'Here's a plan of the house in the story' (giving handouts or showing it on the overhead projector or drawing it rapidly on the board). 'I want you to listen to the story and decide where the man was hiding.' There is obviously little point in beginning the story while some students are trying to work out what they must do. For this reason, it is well worth checking and confirming that everyone has understood.

It is important not to reveal all the ideas for a lesson at the beginning of the period. If in the third part of your lesson you intend to use a picture, do not put the picture on show until you get to that point, so that the students will have something fresh to focus on and their motivation will be helped. In the same way, if you are going to use any handouts, keep them yourself until the time they are to be used. When the time has come to use a handout or a picture make it available/visible to all the students as quickly as possible. Then wait quietly for a few moments so that the students have time to look at it. If you begin speaking at once, many students will simply not listen. They will be preoccupied with what they are looking at, as the eyes almost always take precedence over the ears.

If possible, it is best to move from one part of the lesson to another without allowing a gap to occur, as it is quite difficult to regain the attention of a class, particularly a large one. If you are not very skilled at putting up pictures, writing on the board, using the tape recorder or whatever, it is worth practising (see pages 81–89). You do not want to 'lose' your class while you are fumbling and trying to organise yourself. One way to avoid a gap is to pin up the picture

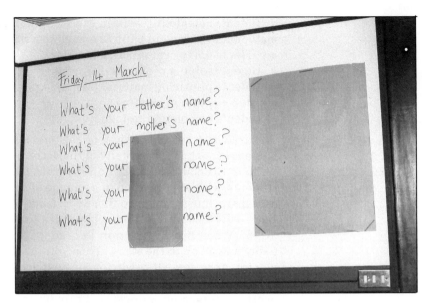

On the image:

Friday 14 March

What's your father's name?
What's your mother's name?
What's your ____ name?
What's your ____ name?
What's your ____ name?
What's your ____ name?

*Words/pictures left covered
until needed*

or write on the board/overhead projector in advance and cover it
with a large sheet of paper that can be removed easily and quickly.
Sometimes you can prepare for the next activity while the students
are busy finishing the previous one. You might be able to write
something on the board, or put a picture up while they are writing.
(But having done this, you need to move on briskly to take advantage of the interest the students show in the new item.) Overhead
projectors are especially useful in this respect because you can
prepare your material in advance and then reveal it to the class bit
by bit. (See pages 81–83.)

Pair work and group work

The amount of practice each student gets is greatly increased by
the use of pair work, and if for no other reason than this, language
teachers should use pair work as a regular part of their classes.
Whilst it is generally agreeable for students to sit either facing
each other for conversation or side by side when looking at the
same book or paper, pair work can be done very successfully simply
by some students turning round or moving along a bit to sit with
a partner. Young learners tend to want to make pairs with their
special friends and this is often perfectly satisfactory. However,

it is a good idea sometimes to vary who sits with whom. To organise this, you need to give a clear directive, e.g. 'We can do this as pair work. Will the front row and Sofia's row please turn round and work with the people behind them.' It is sensible to be more selective about pairing if you are planning an activity which is long, and perhaps difficult for some students. You may wish to try to pair a 'good' student with a less able one, if this can be done without it being too obvious. For quick snippets of oral practice, random pairing which occurs as a result of seating is fine and has the advantage of not interrupting the flow of the lesson too much.

Students soon get used to the idea of pairing, and a simple 'We'll do this in pairs' prompts them to sort themselves out quite quickly and quietly.

Group work tends to occur less frequently but students who have got used to pair work can easily be put into groups. It's often easiest to organise the whole thing yourself. One way is to organise as if for pair work, and then say 'We're going to work in bigger groups, so you three pairs make Group 1, you three Group 2,' and so on. With a class which is used to group work you might say 'We're going to do the next activity in groups. You'll need your notebooks and pens. So take your notebooks and pens and get into groups of six, please. Six to a group. And settle down quickly together,

Group work

please.' A few moments of 'chaos' may follow, but once group work has become a normal part of your class routine, it will not be much trouble.

With group work, it is advisable to say *before* you fix the group size which books, etc. students will need. There does not then have to be a series of return journeys to fetch the necessary items once the activity starts. Some teachers find that having group leaders (different ones on each occasion) and/or giving each group a name (e.g. Group A, Group B, etc.) helps to make the session run smoothly. At first you will probably want to name the leaders, but in time each group can choose its own. Once the groups have been formed, you should give clear, precise instructions about what you want the students to do. Try to give examples of the kind of thing you expect. Indicate how much time they will have to complete the task.

While students are doing pair/group work, you should circulate to listen and to give help where needed. It's best not to spend too long with one pair/group as this sometimes leads to others losing interest in the task as they feel you have lost interest in them. Pair/group work which is allowed to go on for too long causes problems as the students get bored. It's better to err on the side of brevity than risk boredom.

Some teachers may be hesitant about using pair work and group work with very large classes. They perhaps fear that they will have difficulty in controlling the students, and there's no doubt that it can lead to a lot of noise if it is not controlled carefully. For this reason, you may find it useful to explain why you want to do pair work and group work and to impress upon the class the need to behave in a responsible way. On the first one or two occasions when you do pair or group work, you should be especially firm in dealing with noisy or troublesome students. Then you should be able to establish both these ways of working as agreeable and beneficial parts of your lessons.

Ending a lesson

Just as for the beginning of a lesson, there are a few DOs for ending a lesson.

1 DO keep an eye on the time so that you are not in the middle of an activity when the lesson should be ending.

2 DO give the homework towards the end but not in the last few

seconds of the lesson. If you give it too early, some students may try to do it during the lesson. If you give it too late, there is no time to sort out any difficulties. It's often a good idea to tell the class what the homework is and then conclude the lesson with an activity which helps with the task you have set. This gives an opportunity for any problems to be raised and helps to make the students feel confident that they will be able to do the work.

3 DO finish a little early rather than late, even if you have to say 'We'll have to leave the listening exercise until another day. It's almost time for the end of the lesson.' Students will appreciate your courtesy in finishing on time.

4 DO leave the classroom itself in good order—as you would expect to find it. You can ask students to help you—'Carlos, please put the chair back in the corner,' 'Gertrude, please close the window.' It may be normal in your school for a student to be asked to clean the board, but you should ensure that it *is* clean and, if necessary, clean it yourself.

5 DO conclude the lesson, rather than just stop. Say something which indicates that you have finished. You might, for example, refer to what has been done and to what you plan to do next: 'That's the end of the section on "complaining". You should all be able to complain well now!'–and then 'We'll stop for today. Next time we'll go on to "making apologies", that is "saying you're sorry". See you all on Thursday. Bye bye.'

Very often teachers have to hurry away to their next lesson. On the odd occasion when you are not in a hurry (and no other teacher is waiting to come into the room), it is pleasant for the students if you do not rush off. If you take time gathering up your own books, individual students have an opportunity to speak to you informally. You have time to say a few friendly words (in English!) to some of the students as they leave. Of course, you mustn't delay students and make them late for their next lesson.

If you do some of the things suggested in this chapter, you will find that you will be able to control the actual operations in the classroom with increasing ease. Why not glance through the chapter again and mark three or four suggestions which are new to you and which you feel would have the greatest effect on your teaching? Introduce them, one by one, into your work and notice whether they help to make your lessons run more smoothly.

Using audio-visual aids

The range and quantity of audio-visual aids available to teachers varies considerably from country to country and from school to school. Fortunately, the amount of English learned by students is not proportional to the quantity of aids used, so teachers with few resources need not despair! But if you do have equipment and materials available, it is worth making sure that you can use them efficiently and effectively.

This chapter offers some general guidelines on the use of equipment (black/white boards, cassette recorders, video recorders, overhead projectors and so on) and on the choice, preparation and use of materials (recorded tapes, overhead projector transparencies, printed material and so on). It is only possible in this one short chapter to cover a few of the main considerations.

overhead projector (OHP)

cassette recorder

slide projector

video recorder and monitor

The black/white board

Using a board well is a skill which can be developed and all teachers should consider whether their board work can be improved (see Chapter 1, pages 15–17). Here are a few suggestions on how to make your use of the board as effective as possible.

- Write clearly and in large enough letters for everything to be legible from all parts of the class.
- Don't jot words and phrases down at random all over the board.
- Generally avoid speaking at length while you are writing on the board with your back to the class.
- If you ask the students to copy something you have written, stand or sit well away from the board and wait quietly for them to do so.
- Don't use colours which don't show up well on the board (white is best on a blackboard, red is very difficult to see; yellow is hard to see on a white board).

The overhead projector (OHP)

If you have an overhead projector available, you will find, after a little practice, that it is a delight to use. It can do everything a board can do and lots more besides. The two things you need to become expert at are (i) getting the image the right size and in focus and (ii) presenting your information attractively. Again, practice is essential, but don't do your practice in front of a class. A teacher can look very foolish as he or she gets increasingly flustered trying to do what appears to be so simple–making the words, drawings or whatever come into focus. If you wish to practise, remember that to make the image smaller you must pull the OHP itself nearer to the screen, and, obviously, pushing the OHP further away from the screen will enlarge the image. Having got the image the size you want it, you can then focus by turning the focusing knob. If you have not got the space to push the OHP away from the screen you need to use larger writing which means you can get fewer words on the screen.

It is really worthwhile mastering the use of the OHP as you can then enjoy the benefits. You will discover that:

- there is no chalk-dust to put up with;
- while you write you are facing the class;

- material can be prepared in advance;
- material can be kept and used in later lessons;
- you can cover part of what is on the OHP transparency with a piece of paper or cardboard, and present the information as you want it;
- you can go back any number of times to something already used (whereas you may have wiped it off the board).

Preparing material in advance on overhead projector transparencies is arguably one of the most important aids available to you, particularly if you are a new teacher. It means that you can get everything organised before arriving in class and are therefore less likely to make mistakes in front of the students. It assists you in keeping control, because you do not need to turn away from the class to write on the board.

Most teachers use individual transparencies, rather than rolls, for pre-prepared material and store the sheets with their lesson plans or in some other easily accessible system.

To produce good transparencies:

- don't write within 3 cm of the edges;
- put a piece of lined paper under the transparency to guide your writing;

Transparencies – bad and good

- remember that in a large room, your handwriting will need to be about twice 'normal' size;

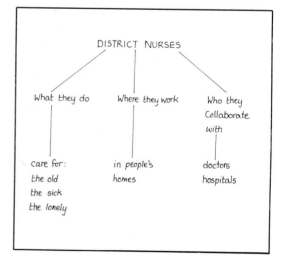

- use different coloured pens to distinguish points (special fibre-tipped pens which are either water-based and can be rubbed off easily, or spirit-based and so less easy to clean off, are needed);
- if you want to use pictures, draw very simple ones or trace outlines, if they are large enough, from books, etc.;
- don't overfill your 'page' (think how few words there are on the most striking advertisements).

Before leaving this section, give yourself a test. Write at least three lines on an overhead projector transparency, then check that you can set it up on the overhead projector and focus it in less than thirty seconds.

The audio cassette/tape recorder

Audio recordings have had a major impact on the teaching of languages and have given students in non English-speaking countries the opportunity to hear English being used for a range of purposes by a variety of people. In addition, of course, audio tapes are used extensively for giving students practice in speaking English themselves.

As for all other equipment, you need to master the operation of the machine before embarking on using it in the classroom (see Chapter 1, page 17).

In Chapter 5, *The classroom itself* (page 54), attention was drawn to the importance of positioning equipment carefully to make good use of the classroom environment. You can choose the location for the cassette recorder by trying it in various positions and varying the volume and tone until you get the best results. You also need to remember to face the speaker on the machine towards the class, even if this means that the controls are inconveniently positioned for you to use.

If the acoustics of the room are poor you can move the students closer to the cassette recorder. It is sometimes particularly appropriate to bring the students into a fairly informal group. 'Gather round and listen to the story' is a natural suggestion and, after the story, students can go back to their places to do the work related to the story.

Choosing audio recordings

There is a great deal of recorded material available from all the major publishers of English material, much of it written in association with coursebooks. So your coursebook may well have tapes/cassettes which you can use in the classroom or in the language laboratory. The teacher's book will almost certainly give guidelines on how to use the recorded material.

Most teachers are not able to choose what material to use. But if you *are* in a position to make that choice, be sure to listen to as large a part of any recording as you can before making up your mind. Consider:

- Is the recording really clear, not just for one person to listen to but for use in a large classroom?
- Is it at the right level for the students?
- Is it easy to use – with clear divisions between exercises and sections and so on, so that you can find the part you want easily?
- Are the links between the recorded material and the related printed material straightforward?
- Does it generate good language work?

CHECKLIST for the selection of audio recordings

Features to consider	Yes/No	Comments
• clarity of recording		
• level of content		
• easy to use (i.e. clear divisions)		
• links with book		
• quality of language work		
• appropriate content		
• culturally acceptable		
• interesting		
• variety of voices		
• agreeable listening		

- Is the content suitable? Are the subjects dealt with 'right' for the students?
- Is it culturally appropriate? Will the students be able to identify with the speakers or at least recognise the sort of people that they are?
- Is it interesting? Will the students find it motivating?

You can use the checklist on page 84 when choosing recorded material for your classes.

Using recorded material necessitates the same attention to preparation as using any other form of material. It is important to make sure that the students know precisely what is expected of them before you begin to play the recording. Are they to repeat? To respond orally? To write something down? Simply to listen and try to remember some points? It is extremely difficult to concentrate on long stretches of recorded material in a foreign language. By giving your students a clear purpose for listening each time, you will help them to keep their attention focused on the task. Fatigue or boredom can set in quite quickly. A listening comprehension passage or a dialogue of about two minutes' duration is plenty for early learners. For oral drilling using a tape recorder, you probably need a break of some sort every eight to ten minutes. A story can last three or four minutes *if* it is interesting to the particular group.

The language laboratory

If your class is working in a language laboratory, most students will be able to concentrate for a little longer. This is partly because they are, as it were, 'alone', and partly because they feel less threatened when they are able to control their own machines and go back if they miss something.

It is important to give your students the opportunity to work at their own pace and in their own way in the language laboratory if you can. Try not to keep on interrupting them while they are working. Your role in the language laboratory is to facilitate learning. You should do what is necessary to assist and support the students, whilst not intervening unnecessarily. You should be ready to:

- organise the setting up of the laboratory if that is normal practice in your school;
- provide a practical solution when a machine is not working;

- restate what the students should be doing if necessary (you will have already given instructions before individual work began);
- monitor the performance of as many individuals as possible, *without* interrupting them if they are getting on well;
- give help to a student who is having difficulty;
- say a word of encouragement or praise to a student;
- stop the whole group and give help or clarification, but only if you find that lots of students are having difficulty;
- answer questions posed by individual students;
- give instructions about what to do next to students who finish before the others (one of the advantages of the language lab is that it allows students to work at their own pace–you therefore need to provide something extra for the faster students to do or be tolerant if they chat while they wait for the slower students);
- draw the lab session to a proper close in just the same way as you would end a lesson in class (see Chapter 7, pages 78–79).

Other audio systems

There are various other audio systems besides the traditional language laboratory which are installed in classrooms in various parts of the world. All have their advantages and disadvantages, their supporters and their critics. Most teachers, however, must simply use the ones they find in their schools.

Whichever system is available to you, the important thing is to be sure you are absolutely 'fluent' in using it. Just as for board-work, you should practise privately before using the equipment with a class. It is time well spent.

Before leaving this section, load an audio cassette into an audio cassette recorder. Test to find the best location for the machine in at least one of the rooms you teach in.

Making audio recordings

Commercially produced material (including some not specifically designed for English teaching) will meet most of the needs of most classes. Teachers generally do not have the time, nor perhaps the technical skill or interest, to record their own teaching material. If you do wish to make recordings, however, you will need to practise using the equipment for recording and, if possible, get some training from someone with expertise. Even if you only wish to make an occasional recording in the classroom, you cannot expect to produce a successful tape without practising.

Making recordings with your students in class can add to motivation, especially if you can make a good enough quality tape for everyone to enjoy. You might consider recording:

- **role play activities:** either using a script, e.g. a dialogue, or asking individual students to act a part.

- **simulations:** this is when students do not pretend to be somebody else, but act as themselves in specific situations–e.g. Student A has got on a bus and does not have sufficient money to pay the fare. Student B is another passenger and tries to help.

- **advertisements:** students, in groups of 2–4, prepare advertisements which are then recorded.

- **school news reports:** students prepare items for a news bulletin and then record them.

- **announcements:** e.g. using the information from a newspaper, students must give 'radio' information on theatre shows, sports programmes, etc.

- **documentaries:** more advanced students can produce sections for a documentary 'radio' programme–perhaps preparing something suitable for other classes to listen to for a special occasion such as the Chinese New Year or Christmas.

Much of the benefit of this kind of activity lies in the communicative use of language during the preparation of the material and the organisation of the recording. With more advanced students, it is a good idea for the students themselves to carry out the entire exercise, seeking advice/help from you only when necessary. An important feature from the learning point of view is that material recorded in class should consist of a number of short pieces so that all the students can be closely involved in some part of the total product.

Using the cassette recorder–whether for play-back or for recording–is not a substitute for giving a lesson. Whilst you may have a few moments' relaxation while a tape is actually playing or while your students are planning their recordings, you must ensure that this work is part of your overall programme for the group and that it is appropriate for that time.

The slide projector

Many schools have at least one slide projector. Geography teachers are often the main users of this particular piece of equipment and, if you want to use it for your classes, you may need to borrow it from that department.

Using slides rather than other kinds of pictures means that you can produce a much larger image which can be seen by everyone in the room. As with all other equipment, it is important to know exactly how to operate the machine before using it with a class. Getting the slides into the holder the right way round needs practice. You will probably find it easiest if you mark all the slides (if they are not already marked) with a small spot or cross in one corner and then always put this mark in the same position as you load the holder.

If other departments in the school have got slide collections, it is worth checking whether you can borrow them and then looking through to see if there are any which you might find useful in your language lessons. You might find, for example:

- that the geographers have a set of slides showing the development of a town. You could use these for short answer practice, or as the basis for the writing of descriptive paragraphs ('Now the town is . . .' and 'In years gone by, the town was . . .');
- that the domestic science department has a collection of pictures of food. These could be used for the practice of lexis, or for making suggestions ('I would cook the chicken . . .' and 'Could you eat the cabbage with. . . . ?');
- that the physics department has slides showing the stars in the sky, which you could use for practising relative positions ('Polaris is nearer to the. . . .'), or as the starting point for a discussion of space travel;
- that the art department has slides of famous paintings, which you might use for exercises on describing people's physical appearance ('He's got a large head') or what they are doing ('The girl is following the woman across the field').

As with all other audio-visual materials, planning and preparation are necessary to ensure that the slides are an integral part of the lesson and not simply an entertainment (although you could, of course, use them in this way at an English club meeting).

The video recorder

Some teachers now have video recorders, and even video cameras, available for their use. The same kind of care must be taken about their positioning and use as for audio systems. If such equipment exists in your school, you should try to get some training, or at least some advice on its use before trying to use it yourself.

There is relatively little specially produced video material on the market, but teachers of English find that they can make effective use of material produced as general television output. You will need to find out what can be used in your country within the laws of copyright, and then to consider whether anything that is available has any potential for your work. If you do have specially published video material to use, it is important to study the teacher's guide with great care as well as making certain that you can operate the equipment fluently.

Video is a powerful tool for bringing the outside world into your classroom and exploits the fact that almost everyone in the world wants to watch television. The teacher, however, must ensure that it is used in pursuit of the learning objectives set for the students and must devise activities based on the material viewed. *Teaching English with Video* by Margaret Allan (Longman 1986) contains

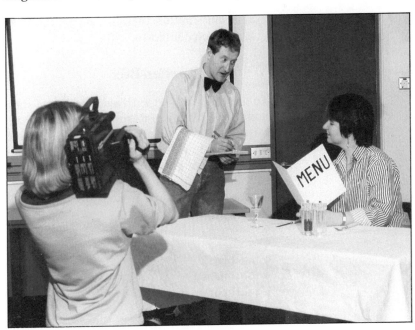

Making a video recording of role play

suggestions about the applications of video to English language teaching, including the use of video cameras in the classroom.

Other English speakers

For many teachers–perhaps for you–the likelihood of having all the sophisticated equipment is small and anyway the prospect of trying to use such things may be daunting. Do not despair! Plenty of people teach foreign languages with nothing more than a board and a book. In any case, you can often provide a wealth of visual aids and occasionally audio aids just by being creative yourself. For example, to supplement your own voice so that your students get used to English spoken by others you might:

- ask other English teachers to visit one of your classes occasionally (in exchange you should offer to visit theirs);
- ask teachers of other subjects (if they speak English) to call in for a few minutes, perhaps to give a short talk on something they are particularly interested in;
- try to bring in an occasional outside visitor–a friend, a representative from a local company–in fact anyone who speaks English (but do decide in advance what they will do when they come, so that they are not embarrassed);
- discover whether there is ever an English programme on radio which you could use.

Your Resources Box

To provide yourself with a collection of simple visual aids, you might like to start a Resources Box. Find a large box, or some other storage system, and into it start to put things you might find useful in your lessons. For things which it is impracticable to store in your box, it's best simply to write sets of words on cards, so that you can collect the things together quickly when you need them rather than having to think of them all over again. You might have a card which reads:

- soap
- flannel
- hairbrush
- toothbrush
- toothpaste
- towel.

Perhaps you would want to collect this set of things together to use in a lesson for talking about habits (using the Present Simple).

Into this same box you can put pictures from magazines and articles from newspapers, so that you have somewhere to look for, say, a picture of an elephant when you want one.

In addition, the box might usefully contain:

- a map of the world;
- a map of your country;
- a map of Britain/Australia/the U.S.A./your nearest English-speaking country;
- a map of your town;
- a plan of a house/apartment (again, a large drawing);
- a train/bus/air timetable;
- a family tree;
- a blank lesson timetable;
- 'realia' such as bus tickets, theatre programmes, letters, envelopes, stamps (all with English language connections).

Some of these could be drawn on OHP transparencies, which you could use over and over again.

It's important to go through the box at least once a year, and to throw out anything which has become out of date or which has proved inappropriate.

Your Resources Box is the place you look when you are asked to take over a class at the last minute, as you can always find something there to 'save the day'.

Having considered all the suggestions in this chapter, you should turn your attention very specifically to the situation in your school. It would be useful to discuss with your colleagues what the priorities are for the development of the use of audio-visual aids in your school. You could consider the following: What is needed? What can be done? Who's going to do it? When?

Reducing the teacher's workload

Teachers will have more time and energy to devote to their students and to their own development as teachers if they can reduce the amount of repetitive work they have to do. This chapter is not a prescription for working less; it offers a few suggestions for saving time which can then be used to better effect. It is not concerned with saving time within a lesson (this is dealt with in Chapter 6, page 67). However, the amount of time you need to spend on preparing and marking will be influenced by what goes on inside the classroom.

Collaboration

The most dramatic saving of time is probably achieved by teachers collaborating in the preparation of materials, although this does mean using some time discussing what to produce. The useful spin-off of collaboration is that it produces an exchange of ideas and gives you an insight into other people's ways of working.

Some teachers are reluctant to work with their colleagues. Perhaps they fear that they may reveal their own weaknesses or that they will be expected to do more than their fair share of the task. You can try to overcome this reluctance, perhaps by offering to lend something you have found useful to a colleague and then, in time, asking 'Have you got anything I could use with Form 2 to teach "apologising"?' or whatever. Or you might offer colleagues access to your Resources Box, on condition that they note down what they have taken and make sure it is returned in good condition.

Simply sharing the job of making charts, lists, etc. can save time, particularly when two or more people find that they are using almost identical material, even if for a variety of purposes.

Saving time by working together

Marking in class

In Chapter 4 (page 43) mention was made of the advantages of getting students to mark their own small class tests, or to exchange with other students for marking. If you feel that your students are getting too casual about this kind of test, you can make them take more care by saying before the test that you intend to take in four or five to look at yourself. You can then collect them in either before they are marked or afterwards. If you take them before marking begins a few students are left with no marking to do when the test papers are exchanged. That doesn't matter, as those students (who won't be the ones whose tests have been handed in) can be called on to assist you with providing the answers.

Giving students help while they are doing written work in class also reduces the time needed for marking. This has the added advantage of the work being less covered with your markings when you return it, which, in turn, makes the students feel less discouraged by their efforts.

Pair and group work

Occasionally, you can ask the students to work in groups of three or four to produce some written work, thus lessening the number of copies you have to mark. This shouldn't be done too often, as it may be that in some groups one student will dominate and do all the work while the rest make very small contributions. It works best if each student has to carry out a small part of the task and then discuss it with the rest of the group before they put the parts together to hand to you. Reports can often be produced like this. For example, if each group is required to produce a report on a football match, they can begin by each student writing a brief paragraph about just one aspect—the weather, the ground, the crowd, the players, the referee, the first half, the second half, the goals, the result, the injuries. Then the group must get together and make whatever changes, additions and deletions are necessary so that the whole thing fits together. This type of exercise involves everybody, allows the better students to help the weaker ones but not dominate them, gives lots of opportunities for group discussion, helps students to see how short pieces of discourse can be joined effectively and, last but not least, leaves you with less marking to do.

Limiting activities

If you are really very tired and under great pressure (perhaps because you've been unwell or doing a lot of extra work), you can get by with minimum preparation for a few lessons (but not many) by working almost exclusively from the coursebook. Students who are used to a more varied 'diet' in your lessons may need to know that you haven't abandoned everything else forever. You could say to them 'I want to get through a couple more units of our book, before we do any more picture stories/games/etc.'

Tired teachers sometimes give a test which fills a whole lesson period, but unless you find marking relaxing or you do it very quickly, you will not gain time, and may lose some, by using this strategy. A test of this length is almost certainly not possible for students to mark for themselves in class, and to be useful it really needs to be marked and returned fairly quickly.

Prioritising your work

There may well be times when you have so many things to do that you don't know what to do first. It is often difficult for teachers to avoid allowing urgent things to take priority over important things. You should occasionally consider whether this is happening to you and what you can do about it.

Priorities differ from person to person and from school to school, so it is a good idea to establish what your priorities are and make sure you have sufficient time to do the important things.

To find the time, you may need, for example, to cut down on the time you spend preparing beautiful audio-visual aids and accept that simpler efforts will serve your purpose. You can, perhaps, train yourself to limit the time you spend on lesson preparation. You may decide that your marking time needs reorganising so that it is spread more evenly throughout the week.

In ways such as these, you will be able to establish a routine and avoid some of the pressure which can build up if you always deal with the 'here and now' matters at the expense of the important ones.

Finally, in the hope of achieving a greater degree of collaboration with your colleagues, make a list of anything you have which you could offer them and a list of the things that you'd love to borrow. Suggest to some of your colleagues that they should do the same thing. Then get together and see if you can help each other. It's a pity not to pool resources if by doing so you can lighten everyone's workload.

Conclusion

This book on *Effective Class Management* has attempted to provide encouragement and really practical suggestions for teachers on the management of their work. It is hoped that by considering the ideas presented here, and perhaps adopting some of them, you will be a more confident and effective teacher with happy and successful classes.

Suggestions for further reading

Only parts (in some cases, small parts) of each book listed deal with topics related to class management.

Baer, E R (ed.) 1976 *Teaching Languages—Ideas and Guidance for Teachers working with Adults.* BBC

Brumfit, C J and Johnson, K (eds.) 1979 *The Communicative Approach to Language Teaching.* Oxford University Press

Byrne, D 1986 *Teaching Oral English* 2nd edn. Longman

Finocchiaro, M 1964 *Teaching Children Foreign Languages.* McGraw-Hill

Harmer, J 1983 *The Practice of English Language Teaching.* Longman

Johnson, K and Morrow, K (eds.) 1981 *Communication in the Classroom.* Longman

Littlewood, W 1981 *Communicative Language Teaching—An Introduction.* Cambridge University Press

Rivers, W M and Temperley, M S 1978 *A Practical Guide to the Teaching of English as a Second or Foreign Language.* Oxford University Press

Smith, D G (ed.) 1981 *Teaching Languages in Today's Schools.* Centre for Information on Language Teaching and Research

Widdowson, H G 1978 *Teaching Language as Communication.* Oxford University Press

Willis, J 1981 *Teaching English through English.* Longman

Teacher's notes and teacher's books accompanying material for class use are a valuable source of ideas for class management.